# BE FIRST

**Being The First To Do Anything Gives You An Enormous Advantage, And You Never Forget Your First**

By Amos N. Johnson

# DEDICATION

To "Bunny": 47 years and counting.

# Foreward

By Theresa "Bunny" Johnson

In 1966 I watched a red MGB come tearing through my flag station at Virginia International Raceway (VIR), scattering the corner workers; who was that guy? Later that day I met Amos Johnson who apologized profusely for scaring us so badly. I watched Amos race in SCCA Regional Races and go to the National Runoffs in 1967, honing his skill, building his engines, loving racing.

In 1967 I watched Amos scratch and fight his way into NASCAR and run a few races, impossible to race on your own dime even in those days.

In 1968 I watched him incorporate a business called Team Highball, Inc. and hire his first employee Dennis Shaw. He was building a team and racing cars and engines for customers. Then in 1969 everything changed in sports car racing when John and Peg Bishop started an organization called IMSA, International Motor Sports Association. This permitted the amateur racers to go professional, seek sponsorships and get paid. What an impact this had on sports car racing.

I watched Amos build his first cars for IMSA, ever improving his driving techniques, attracting sponsorships, racing and winning a lot. First backed by AMC, McCreary Tires, Champion Spark Plugs and many other sponsors. There were lots of ups and downs, unsponsored years, but he kept chasing the next win, the next first.

In 1977 Amos and I walked down the aisle, and he became a husband and stepdad to three sons. He is and was a great stepdad, grandad, great-grandfather and uncle to my huge family. He was simply known as "A", Grandpa A or Uncle A by dozens of kids.

Around 1982, Amos got a contract with Mazda to build a GLC piston engine racer. This started a successful run with them for ten years, racing in two series simultaneously and with so much help from B. F. Goodrich in the RS series and Yokohama in the GTU series. Mazda did more with less than any other manufacturer and they were outstanding in every respect. It was heartbreaking when that program ended.

In 1992 Oldsmobile wanted a new car developed; so, they called Amos and the team to build the Achieva. It was the first GT car built with an aluminum tub chassis.

After racing, I watched him, as Technical Director of two racing series, writing rule books and helping young racers along the way. He still coaches and advises. I watched him learn scuba, get his Master Captain's license, appraise boats, coach young drivers, volunteer 22 years to US Coast Guard Auxiliary, 5 years to FEMA, and 5 years to Lee County Sheriff's VOICE Program.

I've watched Amos for over half a century.

I'm watching him now, writing this book for you, embracing the memories, recalling old friendships and loving every minute. Hope you will enjoy the read……

Bunny

# Table of Contents

1 Mazda 71 ............................................................................. 1
2 Me ....................................................................................... 9
3 TEAM HIGHBALL: ........................................................ 18
4 NASCAR: .......................................................................... 26
5 IMSA: ................................................................................. 31
6 AMC: Gremlin ................................................................. 37
7 AMC Pacer ....................................................................... 51
8 AMC Spirit ....................................................................... 57
9 Mazda Sedans .................................................................. 69
10 Mazda RX7 .................................................................... 81
11 Mazda MX6 ................................................................... 94
12 Oldsmobile ................................................................... 103
13 IMSA: Technical Director ......................................... 115
14 NATCC ......................................................................... 125
15 Rest of Story ................................................................ 135
16 My Career .................................................................... 151
Photography ..................................................................... 157

# 1
# Mazda 71

I woke up when someone kicked my leg, and then I heard someone saying, "Sorry, I didn't see you down there". Rolling out from under the car on a creeper, I realized that I had fallen asleep while trying to figure out how we could route the exhaust from the engine out the right side of the car without setting the car on fire. Before this one, all Mazda racecars had run the tailpipes at least 120 inches, all the way to the rear of the car. It was way late at night in the middle of January 1985, and this new GTU Mazda RX-7 racecar had to be on the track at Daytona in about two weeks for the IMSA 24-hour race, or my goose was cooked.

The 1984 racing season had been a good one. I finished third in points while co-driving with my good friend Roger Mandeville in his IMSA GTO Mazda RX-7; he won the championship. I also gained fifth place for the season with my Mazda GLC in the B F Goodrich Radial Challenge Championship. That was a total of 29 races for the year. Damon Barnett, American Competition Director for Mazda, was pleased, and with Roger's recommendation, he offered me a second contract for 1985 to race an RX-7 in the GTU class in addition to the two-car team of GLCs that I had been running with my teammate Dennis Shaw. I would have two months to come up with a car, and Roger convinced me that it would be better to build my own car rather than buy an existing one. He would be able to help me since he would be racing his same car in 1985. It also happened that the new IMSA rulebook had come out with a few changes. After pouring over the new regulations, I discovered that it was no longer necessary to start with a complete streetcar when building a racecar; we could buy what parts we needed and fabricate the chassis from scratch, i.e. build a "tube-frame" car. Game on: let's buy some parts and get to work.

This new car would be the first IMSA GT car to be built to these new IMSA regulations, not that I had been afraid of venturing out when it came to the rules. Just be careful not to step too far. I had quite a bit of racing under my belt and had, for the most part, built and maintained the cars myself, or at least my team had. Team Highball, Inc. had been an assembly of friends originally, but over the years, it had become a real business with real employees. At this point, with me as President, we had a front office and a shop of fabricators, mechanics and crew, a total of about fifteen, plus any number of people who loved to stop by with a helping hand when needed. Those we called the "elves". My wife, "Bunny", and I had just built a new shop building with two 5,000 sq.ft. Sections to be rented out and Team Highball would occupy the other 7,500. We would be moving in while building the new racecar.

The first order of business had been to order parts. Since I had done some racing with NASCAR, I felt that components for a 3500-pound stockcar would work really well for an endurance racing sportscar. A Southern California company offered a "superspeedway snout" front frame with all front suspension and steering connected. To me, that meant the geometry was all worked out for us. The engine bay for a V-8 should be more than adequate for our 12A, 2 rotor Mazda engine. We would be using a special

Mazda 5-speed transmission, and I would go with a rear-end from Franklin Engineering in South Carolina. They are best known in "round-track" racing for their quick change rear-end, but for us it would be a non-quick-change that would use a ring and pinion gear that they had developed. The gear set was a spiral-cut bevel gear instead of a hypoid gear, meaning less friction and heat and, more importantly, no cooler required. But the pinion comes out from the center of the ring gear instead of lower, off-center. Since the excentric (crank) shaft of a rotary engine is in the center of the engine, as opposed to a piston engine, there would be no alignment problem, just that the driveshaft tunnel would have to be taller. For a limited-slip differential I would go with a Gleason Torsen available from Franklin, again, for less friction.

    Body panels for our RX-7 would be coming from Mazda Competition Department. The few required stock parts we could get from a local dealer or Raleigh Auto Parts junkyard, where we were regular customers. Of course, all these parts ordered would require money. The way our contracts worked with the Mazda factory was Damon Barnett would tell you what was expected of you and how much money Mazda of America would provide. If you agreed, he would send a check for the whole amount and a written contract would follow shortly. It was a simple process. Then, we would have an account with Mazda America Competition where we could order and pay for, whatever parts we needed. If we obtained outside sponsors, that was our own business. There were times when we invested some of our contract dollars in six-month CDs, as the interest rate back then was upward of fifteen percent.

With parts and components ordered, it was time to start building. My fabricators, Bob Hubard and Norm Samuelson, said we needed to build on a sturdy surface plate, so we welded large "I" beams to make a heavy working platform about two feet off the ground. We could attach locating "jigs" where we needed as we welded the chassis pieces together, starting with that front snout when it arrived from California. We borrowed an RX-7 streetcar and made cardboard templates for locating the bodywork and the few stock panels. A stock windshield and roof were mandatory; most all other pieces were fabricated. The racing bodywork was fiberglass and was on the way from Mazda. The car was assembled on the surface plate and then disassembled for painting before finally being finished. The team, with helpers, had just over a month for the whole process.

For the engine, I would go to Roger Mandeville's shop in Spartanburg, SC where he had promised to teach me everything that I needed to know to build my own rotary engines. To help with my new car construction he sent his crew chief, Bob Snow, up to work with my crew. Roger and I go way back in racing. He came from Canada in the '60s to finish college at N. C. State, bringing a Triumph racecar with him. We were in the same sportscar club for several years before he married and moved to Spartanburg, where he built his shop and began racing in IMSA with a Mazda RX-2 and the rotary engine. When first built, they require three hours of break-in running, and I had an engine dynamometer where he could do that. So, he and his wife, Nancy, would come to Raleigh for a weekend visit; the girls could shop, and the guys could work with the engine in my shop. Even though we raced against each other, I helped him with his engines. In a week, he built his engine for the upcoming Daytona race, and he helped me build two engines for my new car. These were 12A Peripheral port rotary engines with a two-barrel IDA Weber carburetor. The horsepower was about 275 with a red line of 9,000 rpm.

By the time I got back to Raleigh Dan Robson and the crew were ready for the engine and transmission to be installed. Ashley Bass, who was a telephone employee by day, had the car's wiring coming along well with special supplies from Bob Akin's Hudson Wire Corporation. Bob had been a friend of mine for quite a while. His wife, Ellen, had been a student at Duke University, and once, when they were dating, Bob had a dental problem, found a local dentist he liked and always came back when he needed a dentist. Because our shop was near the RDU airport, Bob would pop in whenever he came to our area. He had also co-driven with us in a couple of FIA races, winning one of them in our AMC Spirit. With our regular employees Evan Whittles, Marshall McLeod, Dan Upchurch and Rick Thomson working full speed, and with help from the "elves" Chip Snider, James Street and Lloyd Boggs, to name a few, this car was just about finished. We had an automotive paint company down the street in our industrial park that had been painting the bodywork piece by piece. Our shop had been going just about around the clock for weeks, with Bunny, Melanie and others feeding us in shifts from the little kitchen we had put together in the break room. We could see light at the end of the tunnel. There would be no testing; the first time our Team Highball #71 would run would be on the track at Daytona.

When Lewis Curcio and Rick Thomson pulled our trailer into the track infield, there were sounds of relief all around. Damon Barnett and some of the Mazda people were anxiously waiting for us. Yojero Terada, a factory driver from Japan, had been selected as one of my co-drivers along with Jack Dunham, who had been a Mazda RX-7 driver for a couple of years. We missed the first practice while Yokohama tires were being mounted on new Panasport wheels, but each of us managed a few laps the next time the track was open. Qualifying 54$^{th}$ on the grid was just more practice for us; we would be happy to start this race from any position. There were two other Mazda factory drivers there, Katayama and Yorino, to drive with Downing and Mandeville. We beat them both. Yes, at the end of the 1985 Daytona 24 hour race, we were 12$^{th}$ overall and 1$^{st}$ in GTU. What a way to debut this new racer. Team Highball had done it!

# 2
# Me

I was born April 9, 1941, in Garland, a town in the Southeast sandhills corner of North Carolina with about 500 people, mostly farmers. But my dad was their country doctor, Amos Neill Johnson, MD, and my mom was his nurse and lab technician. His father, Jefferson Deems Johnson, or Mr. Jeff as people called him, had built this little town around the house he built for himself on land he had inherited from his ancestors way back in the 1700s. They had come from Ireland for religious freedom, landing in Wilmington and coming up the Black River to settle in what would become the town of Lisbon in Sampson County. I got most of the family history from a book that was printed in about 1940 because my sister, Mary Allan, is on the last page, and I am not even mentioned. Much later, I would learn from Ancestry.com and Family Tree DNA the whole history of the Johnson (Johnston/Johnstoun/Johnstone/De Johnstone) family back into very early Scotland. As a matter of fact, I am a direct descendant of Sir Adam De Johnstone (b. 1420), who distinguished himself at the battle of Sark in 1448. I am one of three Johnsons whose Y-DNA (father-to-son) has been unbroken for that long. If I was in Scotland, I might be recognized as their "Laird."

Neill Johnson is the name I went by for the first 18 years of my life, through grade school in Garland and prep school at The Asheville School for Boys until the computers at Duke University said I was Amos. At Asheville School, I had a penchant for math, which continued at Duke; however, I was sent off to college to become a doctor who should come back home and take over my dad's family practice. As a kid, I was enthralled by cars; I could spot all the newest models as we drove along, and somehow, I found I could listen to the Indianapolis 500 race on the radio. Bill Vukovich was my man. When I started driving, as a 12-year-old, in my dad's '53 Plymouth station wagon hunting car, I spent hours on the dirt back roads behind our home. The Johnson family owned most of the land from Garland to Ingold, 3 miles north, where my great-grandfather, Amos N. Johnson (the first), had built his home and town. No one knew how fast I was on dirt. When I was about 16, my dad took me to Darlington, SC, for the NASCAR Southern 500 race. I watched Curtis Turner in his Ford win, and I was hooked. My sophomore year at Duke was when I got my first car, a 1957 Austin-Healey 100-6. I learned the mechanics required to work on it, and after I turned 21, my junior year, I sneaked off to a Sports Car Club of America drivers' school in Asheville to get my racing license. At Duke, I had been in their sports car club and had won several autocross and had been to races with my friends, Ivan Jones for my first visit to Sebring, FL in 1960, and Jim Kinsler with his Maserati Chevrolet at Marlboro, MD, who would go to work at General Motors, upon graduating, in their Corvette engine research division because of the fuel injection system he had developed for his racecar. It goes without saying my grades at school were falling, and I made the decision to leave school and take care of my two-year military obligation.

    Join the Army and see the world, but, in my case, after infantry training and "jump school," I would spend the rest of my service with the 82$^{nd}$ Airborne running a motor pool at Ft. Bragg in Fayetteville, NC, 42 miles from my hometown. When I arrived there all the troops were on the beaches of Florida waiting to go to Cuba, which never happened. The only other occurrence of interest came when President Kennedy was assassinated. For three days and nights, my outfit slept, fully equipped, under the wings of C124 airplanes, waiting to go "anywhere needed." The short plan would involve parachuting into Washington, DC, landing in the Redskins football stadium. Fortunately, that never happened either. The next thing that never happened was my becoming a helicopter pilot. I would have extended my service to do so but failed my flight physically because of a hearing deficit due to being assigned as an instructor on a machinegun range. That probably saved my life because "chopper" pilots were all in danger in Viet Nam. So, I asked to be released from duty a month early in order to get back into Duke University; I would give it one more try.

  A little older and wiser, I re-entered Duke, but this time, it would be the School of Engineering, not Medicine. My dad was somewhat happier with the decision; he had an older brother, James Wright Johnson, who had been a very successful Civil Engineer. J.W., he was called, had been sent by our government to Russia after the war to help them build hydroelectric power plants. This time, I would stay away from the fraternity life and spend more time with my studies. I would live off-campus, ironically, with three medical student roommates, one of whom had been a best friend from near Garland, Vann Austin. However, I was not giving up cars or racing. When I left the Army, I had saved up some money, enough to buy a new 1965 MGB, the first year its 1800cc engine had 5 main bearings. That was important because I planned to rebuild it for racing. My Austin-Healey had been sold to my brother-in-law in Florida, and, for racing, I had bought a Fiat Abarth 750 Zagato Milano Grand Turismo (double-bubble) from someone in Ohio. After rebuilding the engine, I raced it in S.C.C.A. in H Production. In California, sports car racers had begun modifying their engines for more horsepower, and the MGB modifications had been documented in the *Car and Driver* magazine; therefore, I had the information to follow as a senior project in school. Although my school advisor considered automotive engineering to be a closed subject, I continually went in that direction. When I wrote an essay on "desmodromic valves" I had to convince my instructor that Mercedes had designed and built for racing an engine with that system of valve operation where cams both opened and closed the valves without using valve springs. After two years of engineering studies, with one summer school of physics at N. C. State in Raleigh, I had completed the requirements for the ME degree; however, I was twenty quality points short of graduating because of that sophomore year. I was not interested in attending school another year; I was ready to get on with my life. Along with some of my schoolmates, Hal Byrd, Tom Bobo, and Jim Byrum, we rented a log cabin near Raleigh that we called "Fat City." We played around for a while, taking turns with minor jobs, until one-by-one real jobs separated us. Bobo and Byrd became bankers, and Byrum went to the military, leaving me to get serious about a job.

One Sunday morning, I opened the want-ads section of the *Raleigh News and Observer* and got busy with the search. The first interview I did was for the job of automotive insurance adjuster. They said I could have the job but felt that I was over-qualified and would probably not be happy for long at that work. The second ad I answered was looking for a "hobbyist for interesting work at Bensen Aircraft." I went for the interview and immediately fell in love with the place. This business was building kits for people to assemble their own gyrocopter aircraft, a one-man rotorcraft flyer with a "pusher" engine, as seen in Popular Mechanic magazine and a James Bond movie. Igor Bensen was the President and designer (inventor), and Charlie Elrod was the foreman who could build anything Igor could dream up. They offered me the job starting the next week; I accepted. For the next two years, I punched a time clock daily and worked in every section of the shop. For power, the autogyro used a McCullouch 2600cc flat, air-cooled, two-stroke engine rebuilt from a target drone dug out of the sands of New Mexico. I was the one who modified an automotive Carter YF 1 barrel carburetor for flying. I worked on a crew that helped Igor set 8 world records for autogyro aircraft, and one day, Igor called me into his office to ask if it was true that I built racing engines. I told him yes, and he told me that he needed to try flying with a Volkswagen engine, gave me his credit card and said build him one. The local dealer didn't carry complete replacement engines, but I could order all the parts I needed. It took them two weeks to get my parts, and in about a month, Igor flew my Volkswagen.

He said it was a bit sluggish, but he could tell customers that it could be done.

# 3
# TEAM HIGHBALL:

I finally had to quit punching that clock at Bensen because I was too busy working on mine and other people's racecars. At this point I was doing most of my racing at Virginia International Raceway (VIR), near Danville, VA, considered the home track of the North Carolina Region of the S.C.C.A. since the early '60s. I raced my Austin-Healey, Fiat and MGB there and was a tech official for pro races there. Once, while going through the "up-hills" toward the "Oak Tree" turn, I got off track and ran through a flagging station, scattering the workers, one of whom would become my wife years later. What a story! It was through this amateur S.C.C.A. racing that a group of us got together to share our racing efforts, working on our cars together and partying together. We became a team: myself, Whit and "Bunny" Diggett, Paul and Diny Fleming, Roger Chastain and Roger Blanchard. Dr. Paul Fleming was from Holland and had a Fiat Abarth 1000 sedan; Roger C. was an engineer originally from Florida and had a Triumph Spitfire, Roger B. was from Durham and had a Sunbeam Alpine; Whit Diggett, and Bunny were from Raleigh with an Austin Healey Sprite and I had my MGB. Together, while at a party, we became Team Highball. The name came from the fact that Whit was the North Carolina representative for Old Mr. Boston distillery, but we were not allowed to advertise that. We got together saying that we might not win all the races, but we would win all of the parties. The seven of us were the "terror" of the local autocross circuit. When we went to these parking-lot competitions we would bring home almost all of the trophies. We drove each other's cars and ran in most all classes. Competitors complained that we were using race prepared cars against their street cars; so, Whit and I bought a wrecked MGB from a junkyard, for spare parts, and, before disassembling it, we ran it at an autocross, taking first and second in the class. Whit had a great job. If he could visit the Alcohol Control Board in each of North Carolina's 100 counties once a month, he could set his own schedule. After a while he convinced his boss that they would need to split the state, and who better to take the Eastern half than someone who was born down there - - - Me. That would leave the two of us to advance Team Highball's interests. For a mascot, Roger Blanchard designed for the team a running giraffe wearing a helmet and scarf; he was our resident artist and photographer and the one who came up with "McDo" (spelled make do) because of his anatomical altitude. The proper explanation can be found at a railroad museum in Rockingham, NC. Whistle-stop train stations had over and under lights on a trackside pole; if the higher light was on, the freight train could "highball" it through without stopping.

In 1967, I qualified for the American Road Race of Champions, driving my "B" in National races in both the Northeast and Southeast divisions. That race was held at Daytona Motor Speedway in Daytona, Florida, which would be my first race at what was considered one of the world's top racing facilities. "If You Want to Race, Go to Daytona!" read the bumper stickers. It had been built by Bill France and was the home of the National Association of Stock Car Racing, NASCAR. Unfortunately, I finished thirteenth due to an improperly mounted tire; I even have a photo of that tire to remind me. I had bought myself a new Chevy Camaro for a business car, a 375 hp RS model with a M-22, 4-speed transmission that I also used to pull my race car trailer. On a trip to Alabama for a national race, in the rain, the trailer pushed me off the road and down the side of a mountain. My friend, Lewis Gunter, and I were unhurt, and the MGB and trailer were left on the side of the road. We climbed back up to the road covered in mud to wait, in the dark, for someone to stop. When we heard a car coming, Lewis ran out, waving to the car. Now, Lewis was about 6"4" and three hundred pounds and covered in mud; the car accelerated to get away. I'm sure that started a folk tale about the time Sasquatch tried to attack someone on the mountain. The car was totaled, but when the insurance would not pay me what it was worth, I just had it towed home to Raleigh. I had heard that NASCAR was starting a new category of racing for "Pony Cars", Camaro, Mustang, Javelin, etc.; my car would be rebuilt as a racecar in their Grand American category.

To race in NASCAR was simple. I needed to join as a member, driver and entrant, which I could do because of my SCCA National racing, but to build and race a car you built yourself was a different thing. I ordered a rule book and studied it, following the letter of their regulations. For an engine, I swapped my 396cid "big-block" for the 350cid "small-block" in Whit's Camaro, replacing its crankshaft with one from a 283cid to bring the displacement down to the five liter size required. I was able to buy a camshaft and some used pistons and connecting rods from famous North Wilkesboro, NC, car builder Junior Johnson. Just going to

Junior's race shop was a "trip"; in the building behind his and Flossy's home, surrounded by a little white picket fence, was one of the winningest racing facilities of NASCAR. One room there had only some chairs around a table where Junior and his local friends played checkers most afternoons. To my completed engine I added a Holley 850cfm carburetor on an Edelbrock aluminum manifold and had the engine I needed. I had been building four-cylinder MGB engines and even a Volkswagen engine that flew, so the V-8 engine was not a problem. Car finished, load it up and go to Jefferson County speedway in Georgia. NASCAR's Bill Gazaway and his brother Joe looked the car over and asked what rear-end that was and what front hubs they were. Well, the regulations said the big Holman and Moody Ford parts were optional; so I had stayed with my Chevrolet parts. They said that I could not do that. There were a few other things I would have to change also but they said that I could take one lap behind everyone and then take my last place prize money and go home. And, go over to Buck Baker's car and tell them Bill Gazaway sent me to look at the way his car was built. It took more time and money, but I would wind up racing with them later, and one Sunday morning at Hickory, NC speedway, the NASCAR officials came to me before the race saying they had a sticker to put on my car: "Official NASCAR Racecar"!

1968 was a busy year for my racing effort. In addition to the NASCAR Camaro and the SCCA MGB someone I had met at a Grand American race, Fred Opert, offered me the use of an Elva Courier that he had. It was a right-hand-drive, fiberglass Sebring model that raced in the

D production class, or at least it would if I put one of my MGB engines in it. I could race it all year and then give it back, in running condition, at the end of the year. One SCCA National race weekend at VIR, I raced all three of the cars: MGB in E production, Elva in D production and Camaro in the A sedan class. By the end of that year I had qualified all three cars for the American Road Race of Champions to be held at Riverside Raceway in California. There was no way to get all three cars across the country for that, but I would take two of them. My good friend Lewis Gunter and a friend of his would drive my Dodge van out, towing the Elva, and I would drive the MGB across the country with a stock engine in it. Once there, we could put my racing engine in it for the competition. After the races, Fred Opert would take the Courier back and Lewis could bring the MGB home on the trailer. That would leave me in California with a bit of time to go to a Jim Russel Formula Ford driving school to see if I might be interested in racing formula cars. I decided "no"; I liked having four fenders around me! That whole plan worked out in the end, but my engines did not like running on SMOG, and I finished an unbelievable thirteenth in both of my races. The good news was that we managed to get my cars and engine back across the border when Lewis and friend had decided to detour into Mexico on the way out!

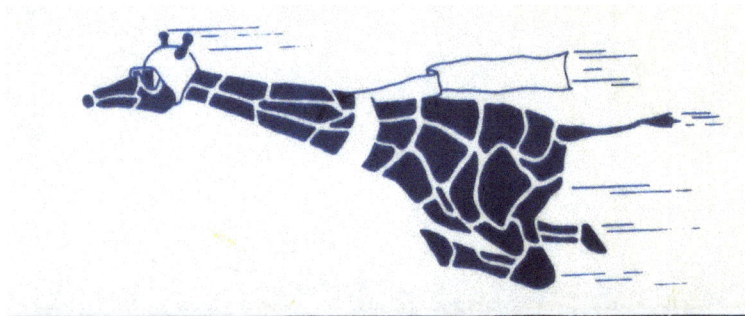

# 4
# NASCAR:

For 1969 I would spend most of my time racing the Chevy Camaro, and the majority of the races were on short oval tracks where it was really a learning process. I had made a friend of Richard Childress from Western NC. He had one mechanic with him most of the time, and I had my friend Chuck Ryan with me. Chuck had been crazy enough to go with me the year before when I drove my MGB across the country to Riverside. Childress had an old Orange Crush drink truck as his transporter, and I was flat towing my car behind my Dodge van. Smokey Yunick had come up with a way to flat tow a stock car using cables and pullies to have the car steer behind you with a towbar. The full floater rear end allowed you to pull the axles out to protect the transmission and rear end. It's not an ideal setup, but inexpensive. We ran at South Boston, VA, a couple of times, then Charlotte Motor Speedway and to Daytona for the July 4 race. I was not doing too well, but I was finishing better than where I started. We went on the "Northern Tour," a series of about six races in a row up North. At one of the tracks, Childress crashed through the guardrail and I blew up an engine; so, I helped him repair his car, and he loaned me an engine to get to the next race. We finished the cars and started out late at night, only to have someone crash into my racecar while towing. He was a disabled veteran driving with hand controls, and I couldn't shoot him as I felt like doing. Richard went on to the race and I missed that one while I settled with the insurance company. I made out pretty well, dollar wise; I made more than I would have made in prize money. The car was looking pretty bad, though, and I would put new 1969 bodywork on it when I got home.

We raced at Stafford Springs, CT, Oxford, ME and Thomson, NH. I lost another engine and replaced it with one from a junkyard. The only one I could find was a stock 283cid, and I told that to Joe Gazaway, our NASCAR Tech. He thought I was pulling his leg and went along and "pumped" it anyway, then said I must be too dumb to cheat. They had a way to measure the volume of one cylinder through the sparkplug hole and then multiply by eight to get the size of your engine. Once done, they sealed the engine with a wire seal from a manifold bolt through a stud holding the carburetor on. If you ever broke the seal to replace an engine, you had to get the new motor checked. Since that was an unnecessary nuisance for me, I devised a way to undo the seal and then put it back, not to cheat, but to save time and trouble. But I had all the parts with me to build another engine, or at least I thought. With a race at the new Michigan International Speedway coming up, we planned to stop in Cleveland at Chuck's dad's home to work on the car. I got all my parts out for my engine and found that the piston rings were not the right ones for the new pistons. What a predicament! Johnny Boyette at Boyette's Automotive in Raleigh had let me down. I called every place I could think of trying to find a set of Clevite 77 dykes rings - - wait a minute - - - Clevite!!! They're made in Cleveland, OH. Chuck's dad said no problem, and he took me over there. I explained the whole problem, and they found what I needed; however, they had no way to retail any parts. Fortunately for me, word had gotten around that a racer was there with a problem, and a PR man showed up. He had my piston rings in one hand and the dykes rings in his other. He said it was not a problem, switched them around and handed them to me saying have a nice race! That turned out to be a very strong engine. I had always built my own engines, making better horsepower by paying attention to detail. Richard Childress had used factory Chevy Z-28 engines without reworking them. He didn't run them hard; they were not as strong and lasted a lot longer. That engine I had borrowed from him for a race he said had seventeen races on it. Well, I liked to go faster. At Michigan, with my new engine, I would qualify third behind longtime NASCAR drivers Tiny Lund and Pete Hamilton and ahead of Buck Baker. I was the fastest qualifier on Firestone tires. Waiting for the start, the Firestone people took good care of me by putting sunshades over my windshield. The race started and I was running right with those veterans up front. Buck Baker tried to pass, but I held him off. Twenty-one laps into the race, still in third, I come by the pits and give Chuck a thumbs-up, and the engine blows up! It was great fun while it lasted, and it showed that my car and I could run with the "big boys."

  Back home, I built another engine and put a better oil cooler on the car. I also bought a used truck and built a ramp on it to carry my car. Believe it or not the next race is on a dirt track at the Raleigh State Fairgrounds. I finally got my car out there in time to qualify. Ken Piper, NASCAR director for this series, and his wife couldn't believe I was that late to show up. They were always trying to put on the best show possible, telling us when we needed haircuts and asking us to dress our pit crews better. They were good people. This would be a hometown race for me and my first and only dirt-track race. I qualified in the top ten and was running there, but the track was giving up, and the dust was so heavy I could hardly see to the next turn until I saw the front end of another car just before I hit him nose to nose. My race was over, but at least it wasn't a long trip home.

The car was easily repaired, and in a couple of weeks, it was off to the Talladega Speedway in Anniston, Alabama, for my first superspeedway race. I was late getting there as usual, had trouble with the car and never made it into my Saturday race. That was the first race ever on the new track there in Anniston, AL. The Grand American 400 on Saturday and the Grand National 500 on Sunday; however, the first line Grand National drivers, as a group, decided not to race because they said the track was too fast for the tires that were being used. They could only go about four laps wide open before the tires were used up. Big Bill France said he had thousands of spectators on the way to see this first race on the longest and fastest track in the country, and he was going to have that race on Sunday. He came down to the Grand American paddock and personally invited us to drive in the 500 mile race the next day. And my car was ready to race! A few of the non-factory Grand National cars would race and a few of our drivers would move up to race them, but I definitely wanted to race my car in his race. I had good old Chuck and a couple of house painters who had come with us from Raleigh. Between my crew and Childress' people, we could handle pit stops. In a race like that, I would not actually race against anyone; I would keep my car running as smoothly and safely as I could, paying attention to my gauges to make sure that the engine would make it to the end. I would run wide open and draft other cars if my engine temperature was good, but after five or six laps, I would have to break the draft and give the engine a rest. That plan worked, and while Richard Brickhouse went 500 miles to win, I went more like 400 miles to finish 13$^{th}$ overall, 6$^{th}$ in class and ahead of Richard. The biggest payday of my NASCAR career and a feather in my cap. A week after that race I got a letter in the mail from Bill France saying thank you for the support, and if I ever felt NASCAR was not treating me well, to use the letter as a reminder.

# 5
# IMSA:

It was about this time that we began hearing rumors that an unhappy SCCA big wig named John Bishop had approached NASCAR president Bill France with an idea to start a professional road racing series for "sporty" cars to be named International Motor Sports Association (IMSA). That would be right up Team Highball's alley. I was ready to get back into road racing after spending a couple of years on oval tracks. We found out who to contact and were able to sign up as new members and have a regulations package sent along with a list of cars. There would be four categories: Sports Cars, over and under 2.5-liter displacement, and Touring Cars, over and under 2.5-liter displacement. But to get started, the first race would be held at Talladega, Alabama for cars called International Sedans with rather open rules based on FIA sedan regulations but including most SCCA sedans as well as those built to European rules. Whit and I found a lightly crashed Opal Kadet in our local junkyard that could fit the touring category, and we started building. This car would be the first car built to IMSA rules, and we would try to take full advantage of that. Throughout my whole career in racing, I have taken advantage of the rules. That means finding any loopholes and grey areas to use for an advantage. We would never cheat!

It was a rag-tag group of cars that made it to Talladega for that first race: Datsun 510, Austin Mini, Fiat 124, Alfa Romeo, Renault, VW, BMW and our Opal Kadet. There were two English Ford Cortinas of special interest.

Big Bill France and his son, Little Bill, had found that there were a few "slightly wet" Cortinas that had come from a sinking ship from England, available from Holman and Moody in Charlotte. Stockcar builder "Tiger" Tom Pistone prepped two for the France family to race. The deal was that the loser of the two would have to pay for the cars. It was a fun weekend. On practice day, Big Bill stayed in his car and had a hotdog for lunch because "Tiger" Tom had welded the doors shut, and it was too difficult to get "Big" Bill in and out of the compact car. I do not know who paid for the cars, and our Opal did not finish the race. But Team Highball was there for that first IMSA race, and there was prize money.

That Fiat 124 sedan in the first IMSA race had been built as a NASCAR Grand American series under 2.5-liter category that had not been a successful effort. So, it had been a ready to go early IMSA car. Our Highball teammate, Dr. Paul Fleming, bought it and had it delivered to Raleigh. In 1970 it was a perfect under 2 liter FIA entry for the Daytona 24 hour race. This car required very little additional preparation to race in that world famous endurance race. I had help from a Raleigh native, Bill Barnes, who happened to be a commercial tool and die maker as well as an excellent race driver and mechanic. He had been involved in SCCA's Trans/Am racing series with an Alfa Romeo and had, long ago, raced sprint cars on board tracks. He could fabricate anything and drive anything, and he would be the third driver, along with Paul and me. The February 1970 FIA race at Daytona would be the first of many endurance races for me and would be a great learning experience. In these long races, you don't want to actually race against another car; you race against the track. Yes, drive fast, but take care of the car, and since you are in a slower class, watch your rear-view mirrors so that you don't get hit from behind by the faster cars. Our little Fiat ran trouble-free for 24 hours, earning us first in class and sixteenth overall for our first race. A month later, we would take it back to Florida for the 12-hour international race at Sebring, a race that I had been to as a spectator or track worker every year since 1960. Just to be on that track racing was beyond belief for me. However, about halfway through the race, while running trouble free, Paul was "black-flagged" (called into the pits by the officials) and told by the chief steward to take the car behind the pit wall. He was blamed for causing the crash of one of the faster cars. By the time we were able to convince the official that they had the wrong car, we had been disqualified for "going behind the pit wall". Ironically, the car that caused the crash wound up winning our class. That official was never again one of my favorites.

    The weekend had been very interesting and memorable for other reasons, and a book was even written about that particular race by a friend of mine, Harry Hurst. It turned out to be a very close race to the finish between Mario Andretti in a Ferrari and Peter Revson in a Porsche. Mario's Ferrari had broken early, and near the end, the team put him in another car that was running in second place to see if he could catch the Porsche, and he did, right at the end of the race, winning the 12-hour race by less than a minute. Revson's car was co-driven by the actor Steve McQueen, who had been driving with his left foot in a cast. I can attest to that because earlier in the week, early one morning, as I was working on our Fiat, McQueen rode up on a mini bike. He was enjoying riding around the paddock without spectators bothering him. He stopped to see the racing seat that I was installing and told me it was one from a business of his, Solar Products, and wanted to make sure I was mounting it properly. I would see him several times later because our pits were adjacent. Once, one of his crew brought some rope over for us to put up on the other side of our pit; I asked why beyond our spot, and he said if we didn't, fans would be standing in our area to try and see Steve. He was right, and when Paul allowed one young lady to cross our pit to peek around the separating wall, she found herself face-to-face with Steve McQueen! "OH, he's got sideburns!" was her response. After our disqualification, we had ring-side seats for the finish of that race.

In 1971, Paul, Bill and I would return to Daytona's 24-hour race with an improved version of the Fiat sedan. It was faster, but a new FIA qualifying rule kept us out of the race. As a matter of fact, that qualifying speed regulation kept all the U-2.0 class cars out. Paul was mad, so he bought a Corvette with a 454cid engine to take to the Sebring 12-hour race. Unfortunately, we had little time to prepare and blew a head gasket to end our FIA effort. After that, IMSA became the controlling organization for the endurance races which meant we would be dealing with different classes and regulations.

IMSA racing continued in 1971 for Team Highball with an International Sedan race at our favorite track, VIR, in Danville, Virginia. My Opal, with Roger Mandeville as co-driver, finished first in TU, 12$^{th}$ overall, and Paul's Fiat finished second in TU, co-driven by Theresa "Bunny" Diggett, IMSA's first female driver, and she happened to be Dr. Paul's office manager. I would race the IS Opal two more times, back at Talladega for sixth place and at Charlotte Motor Speedway for fourth place.

Away from IMSA and SCCA we had found in Western NC a man, Bill Ellis, who had been a NASCAR racecar builder and now had started a racing series for compact cars. Most of it would be on oval tracks, but he had built his own little road course utilizing part of an eighth of a mile drag strip. He accepted my Opal to run in its first race, and I won the pole and the race.

At the VIR race, IMSA introduced a new racing category, Baby Grand, which was a throwback to the NASCAR connection. Those cars were less modified cars racing on street legal tires with two classes, "B" and "A", based on engine size, and I would park the Opal to move into that series with a Ford Pinto. Without much modification, I made it to the race at Summit Point, West Virginia and finished 18$^{th}$ overall and 8$^{th}$ in class "B". I had the chance to sell that car, so I started studying the rules and decided to try the American Motors Gremlin, which had the largest engine in that "B" category. The Gremlin had just been introduced by AMC, and I would have to bite the bullet and buy a new one.

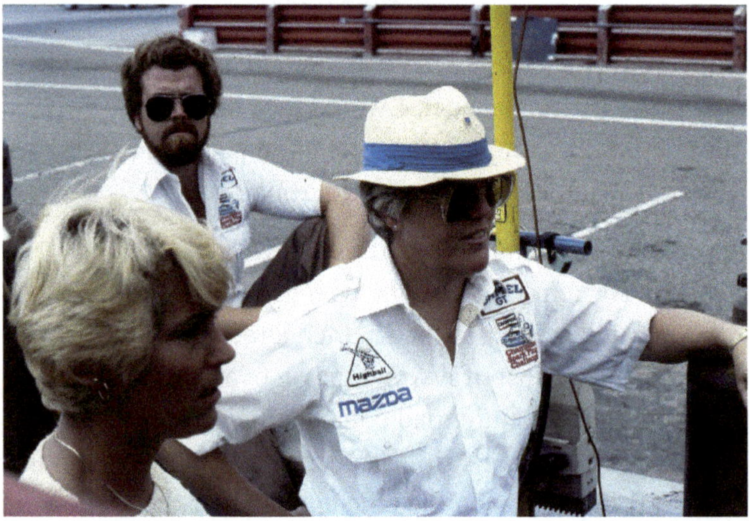
Highball
mazda

# 6
# AMC: Gremlin

To race in IMSA's Baby Grand category "B", the fastest of the two classes, Whitney and I had decided we would go with the car with the largest engine, a 232 cubic inch six cylinder. It also meant we would have the largest and heaviest car, but the engine's torque should take care of that if we could just get the funny shaped car to handle the curves. There were commercials for the Gremlin that said, "Hey lady, where's the rest of your car?" because there was nothing but a bumper behind the rear wheels. That would be a challenge, and we would be the first to put this car on the racetrack. I went to Raleigh's AMC Nash Rambler dealer with a plan and the best salesman you could imagine. By the time Whit finished, we had bought the ugliest new green compact 1970 car you have ever seen for $1,800. They were probably dancing to rid themselves of that car, and we let them keep the interior; it would be stripped out for racing. I had never worked on a new car before; it was so clean. We put a roll cage in it and replaced the standard gas tank with a safety fuel cell. Next, the engine came out for a racing rebuild. It got its ports enlarged, a racing valve job, and we milled the head 0.100" (that's a lot) to get more compression. We did not have time to have the camshaft re-ground for racing, and no one sold one for this engine, but looking at the valve timing specifications, I thought the engine might perform well if I advanced the stock cam 8 degrees with an offset bushing. We found an exhaust header for sale in a J. C. Whitney mail-order catalog. It was made by an AMC dealer in Mesa,

Arizona, and they would later become one of our valued sponsors. "6=8" Clifford Research was their ad. And finally, we came to the carburetor. Remember that my first real job had been with Bensen Aviation, building gyrocopter kits. Their engine had run with a Carter YF 1 barrel carburetor, and here it was on our AMC 232 six-cylinder engine; I could make those things fly!

We reassembled the car, lowering it with shorter, stiffer springs and fitted new stiffer shock absorbers and anti-sway bars front and rear. A trip to a truck stop's scale showed that we needed to add weight to be legal; so we put that weight inside the rear bumper to help make up for the lack of rear bodywork. I would drive Team Highball's new racing AMC Gremlin from Raleigh, NC, to Daytona, FL, to break in the newly rebuilt engine. Then I put a number "7" decal on it and raced it in the Daytona 150-mile race, finishing third in its first race. Success, you bet! Now, let's trailer this one home and build another one for Whit.

We found a slightly damaged Gremlin that we could repair for a second team car. I also came up with a camshaft and did a little more work on the Carter carburetors. Both cars got the Red, White and Blue paint job, and we added our new sponsor's logo, LEVI'S. Whit had done his thing: a little money and clothing for our whole team for the 1972 season. Once you get a few sponsors, others will want to be a part of your winning team, so we added Shaeffer clutch and flywheel, Hurst shifters and Thiokol brake pads. The deal with most of them was that we got product and, when we won, a monetary reward. He also had come up with a tire sponsor for us. All cars had to race on steel legal tires, any size that would fit on the standard wheels. He found a small company in Pennsylvania, McCreary, that manufactured their own tires as well as tires for other brands. Joe Jacobs was our contact there and he would fly himself and a tire engineer to each of our races, and we won races for them for a couple of years, even when B. F. Goodrich took over the series and named it the Radial Challenge. Joe told us that he knew the day would be coming when BFG would have to have us race on their tires, and he would gladly thank us and help us make the change over. He was right. Gary Pace of Goodrich, said whereas he could not officially sponsor our team, he would be able to choose us to do tire tests and put tires on all our vehicles. He was from Eastern North Carolina and had distinguished himself with the Akron, Ohio, company by his energetic approach to performance tires. He opened a connection with us that would go on for more than ten years, including a one-time BFG/THB golf tournament that was great fun.

There were only six IMSA Baby Grand races in 1972, and I won my first at Brainerd, Minnesota, where Whit finished third. Someone told me that up there, if summer fell on a Sunday, the people would all have a picnic; it was way North, and the mosquitos were fierce. The first two races had been Bryar, New Hampshire and Daytona, won by Carson Baird's Ford Pinto and Earl Fellin's BMW as Whit and I still had sorting problems. At our home track, VIR in Virginia, I was third, and Whit was fourth; Carson Baird won. At the fifth race, Watkins Glen, New York, a Pinto won again. But for Team Highball, that was still a big year. We were a two-car team with sponsors, and when Whit won the last race at Daytona, we were both winners.

It was also a great year for IMSA, as the fledgling business took over from the Federation of Automobile Racing (FIA) in France, running professional road racing in America. John Bishop, along with his wife Peg and help from Bill France's NASCAR, was showing the success that would build an international organization. And Team Highball was doing its part to help by building race cars and promoting the Baby Grand class alongside the IMSA Grand Touring class. There were as many as 30 cars in our races, and would ultimately be as many as 75 cars running for the championships.

February 1973 began for us in a storm, a snowstorm of historic proportions that dumped 23 inches on the South between Raleigh and Daytona just days before our race weekend. I called the Highway Patrol to ask the best way to drive South to Florida and they said don't go. Since we had to be there for this first race of the season, we loaded one car in the truck and the other on a trailer behind it, taking the Interstate 95 highway as the best choice. In South Carolina, we had to drive on the shoulder of the road several times to get around cars abandoned on the road. We saw where people had burned their spare tires for warmth. At one intersection travelers had hiked to a motel under construction to take refuge. Our joke was that for the snow removal crew, there must be two shovelers and a wheelbarrow. The trip took 27 hours, but we finally arrived at the Daytona Speedway for the first race of our season, the IMSA Citrus 200, which was a preliminary race for NASCAR's Daytona 500. As it would turn out, each year for many to come, IMSA would have three races at the

Daytona Speedway, February, July and November, and I would have great success there beginning in 1973.

At Daytona, there was a 3.8-mile-long infield road course inside the 2.5-mile stock car track. During qualifying, as I ran down the back straight into the banked NASCAR third turn, I saw two people looking down on the track from a point where there were no spectators allowed. I couldn't believe my eyes; my father and Bill France were those two people! I would find out later that my dad was on the board of directors of Dr. Murdock Head's company, and he was on the NASCAR board of directors. Dr. Head had flown down from Virginia, picking my dad up in North Carolina on the way. So, after a first of the season win in the Citrus 200, when I was taken up to the press box, there was my father with Bill France and Murdock Head to greet me for the celebration. Oh, my teammate, Whit, finished second in the race and Levi's had sent a representative to check on us. He brought with him a pair of blue denim car covers made to fit our cars with hip pockets for the Gremlin's flat, unusual rear. What had started miserably turned out to be a great weekend, and we were off to a winning year as I would win all three Daytona races in that eight-race season. At the year-end banquet, I received a 1973 IMSA Baby Grand Championship trophy.

The Dr. Murdock Head connection was quite a story. He was a medical doctor and dentist, as well as a lawyer, but he didn't practice either; he made documentary films and ran his business called Airlie Foundation Conference Center from a town he had bought, Airlie, Virginia, just outside Washington, DC. All this small town was used for conference meetings by organizations in some way connected to our government. I knew of him because he had visited my home in North Carolina to film my dad, who had, through his medical practice, somewhat specialized in arthritis treatment. Dr. Head would fly down, buzz our house and then land the private plane at a landing strip nearby. His pilot was his sound and cameraman. My father had been added to the board of directors of Airlie Foundation. After our meeting at the Daytona race, he invited me to visit him in Virginia. He had a stretched limousine that needed some special work. I flew up and was picked up at a DC airport by his driver in the limo, who delivered me to Murdock's home at Airlie. I was told to go in and back to the kitchen and would be fed breakfast before meeting with him. There was someone there also having breakfast, Marty Robbins, the singer, who had crashed in a NASCAR race, injuring his face. Dr. Head was having a plastic surgeon work on him. Then I was told to go upstairs, to the room on the right, where I found Murdock still in bed with a telephone at his ear. There in the same room, on a massage table, was Bill France, and at a desk, there was U.S. Secretary of State Melvin Laird, talking on another phone. I would not have been surprised to find Jesus Christ in that room, too. Finally, I would talk with Dr. Head; he made me an offer of sponsorship to race in NASCAR, but I would have to move my shop to Airlie and take care of all his vehicles, too. I did the work on his limousine for him, but two weeks later, when I returned it, I had to tell him I couldn't accept his sponsorship offer; I was just too tied up with IMSA road racing.

    Back in Raleigh, over the winter, big changes were underway. First, Whitney decided to sell his car and retire from racing; he had too many responsibilities to give up his job and go racing full-time, and that seemed where we were headed. That meant I would need help and a shop. At Daytona I had come to know a young man (18-year-old) from Raleigh who was a mechanic at a dealership and a beginning racer, Dennis Shaw. I went to see him and wound up hiring him as my first paid employee. I still had help from several people on the side, notably Joe Purcell, who was a long-time friend who would do anything I needed done. I also had a roommate, Wolfgang Christian, a student at N. C. State College, who had partnered with me to buy a home in Raleigh. We had the house on half of the one-acre site with room to build an oversized, free-standing garage. So, I ordered a garage kit and built it myself with help from Dennis, Joe and Wolfgang. We were now Team Highball, with a shop.

Along with building the shop, we were able to build a second Gremlin for B. F. Goodrich. Gary Pace had come up with an idea and money, for filming the Goodrich Radial Challenge races. He would have me build another Gremlin that would be driven by celebrity Brock Yates and would be a camera car, filming from within the race. IMSA liked the idea and would allow us to make some performance options beyond the rules so the cameras could be where needed to cover the races. It would not be in the competition. All cars for 1974's 8-race season would now be in one class and would be called "RS" (racing stock). IMSA was expanding and would add the West coast to its racing venues with races at Ontario Speedway and Laguna Seca near Monterey, California. My season would not be as good as the previous year, but Dennis and I would pick up a win in the six-hour endurance race at Mid-Ohio Raceway in Mansfield, Ohio. The engine failed with one turn to go, and I coasted across the finish line with the victory. We picked up Dick Holland AMC Jeep as a sponsor not just for that race but for later years, too. He would always let us work on our cars at the dealership and, of course, display them to the public. We would maintain the "TV" car for Brock and even drive it a few times. The camera in that car was huge, and the film would have to be changed several times in a race. My #7 Gremlin broke at the Atlanta race; so I drove the "TV" car for the last part of the race and was able to cover Nick Craw's BMW from the track as it took the checkered flag. After BFG had all the film they needed, they let us put #11 on the car with Dennis racing it. Their films came out well: "Racing the Radial Challenge" and "Decision at Daytona" can still be found on YouTube. In the latter film, you would see that at the Daytona Finale, I could have won the race but backed off on the last lap to allow another Gremlin racer, George Alderman, to win, securing the championship for him and AMC. Sometimes you do the right thing.

We were back to being a two-car team for the '75 season, plus we had hired another mechanic, Bill Brown, who had started building his own Gremlin. He said he was paying his bills to build a car and go racing; so if I wanted to pay him to do the same thing, count him in. And I hired a crew chief for the team, Jim Woodward. There were two other cars being built in the Raleigh area by Ed Allen and Steve Coleman, who would co-drive with me in a couple of races. We had really started something with AMC. Their competition manager asked me to send our car hauler to the factory in Kenosha, Wisconsin, and it came back with five Gremlins on it that had been used for testing. We could build and sell them for racing. The builder in North Wilkesboro was able to acid dip a body and put a roll-cage in it in about a week's time to start the process, and we would go ahead and do the preparation even without a buyer. Every car we built would be slightly better than the one before; so we put our numbers on with decals, and I would take the newest. Then Dennis made his choice and some of the others would be available for sale or rent. We had drivers that rented our cars by the race. Les Delano, Andy Petery and Steve Whitman all worked in New York City, and racing with us was their get-away time. There were times when people like the Whittington brothers from airplane racing wanted to go racing in IMSA's 24-hour race but had no racing license. John Bishop said to call Amos and rent one of his cars for the preliminary race. In that instance, our rental cars were taken; so they bought one. It wound up being used by several of their friends who wanted to race. Our results for the ten races that year were two wins for me, Daytona and Road Atlanta and two for Dennis, Sebring and Talladega. We would also do several tire tests for Goodrich.

By this time, IMSA had realized that the AMC Gremlin might be too competitive, and they mandated a restrictor plate to go under our good old Carter YF carburetor to slow us down a bit. Thus began a game between us and IMSA's competition director. Dennis and I would use our Dyno to find a way to get the power back, and he would then say we couldn't do it that way. We would go back to work on it until we finally found a legal way that he could not stop. Almost all racing uses restrictions to try and even out the competition, and all teams look for ways to overcome the power loss. There was one longer 6-hour race at Mid-Ohio where we put another Gremlin on the track with additional sponsorship from Levi's for Gals, an all-girl team with well-known drivers Toni Creighton and Janet Guthrie. On practice day, as we were all having lunch, no one could find Janet. We finally located her sitting in the car, mentally taking more practice laps. That was just Janet, and she would go on to race in both NASCAR and Indy Car. They didn't win, but they had a good race. One time, while making one of our twice a year trips for the West Coast races, we had a flat tire on our motorhome in the middle of nowhere Arizona and pulled off in a deserted service station. While wondering what to do because it meant changing a rear spare to a front wheel, we looked up to see the BFG racing services truck pulling off the highway. Buddy Ankrom and Frank DeAngelo, laughing, said no problem. They cranked their generator and compressor, changed the tire and had us on the road in no time, just ahead of a storm. That's what friends are for.

    Levi's was a good sponsor, and I had the best relationship with their advertising manager, Bud Johns. When I found out that he was coming to our race at Lime Rock, Connecticut, I couldn't decide whether to cut off the beard I had worn for a few years. It was a moot point; he had a beard and a ponytail. I should have known; the Levi's offices are in downtown San Francisco. Once, when we were racing out there, I visited Bud at his office, and he took me to a room with more clothing on racks than you can imagine. He said that I was about the same size as their model and if I saw anything I liked, I should take it. When a clothing manufacturer had something that they wanted Levi's to market, it would be sent to Bud for approval, with a small tag with a carrot replacing the little red Levi's tag. "Fresh Produce," they called it. I would not only take a few items then, but for the next eight years, I would not buy any clothing other than my underwear. Levi's outfitted me with everything they made, work, casual, dress and formal; I became a Levi's man. There was an annual clothing manufacturer show in Huston, TX, where they all show off their new items to dealers. Bud had me come there to be with him; I was his show! He had a slot-car racetrack set up with signs "Be First with Levi's" and pictures of my Gremlin with its LEVI'S decals. He offered buyers the chance to race against his "Champion," and if they won, they got a pin with a blue ribbon that said, "I Beat Amos Johnson." I was there wearing a new Levi's leisure suit, a tan one on Saturday and a blue one for Sunday. It was great fun and a great stop for Bud's customers. He pulled me aside once to tell me that they wanted to see some of those ribbons out in the crowd, so maybe I should let someone win. I had the chance to "hang" with a few other celebrities there, like football hall of famer Joe Montana. Just saying! It was an adventure for me, but back to business. As I usually did, with IMSA's approval, I built next year's car and raced it at the Daytona finale; we would be the first team to race the new 1976 AMC Pacer.

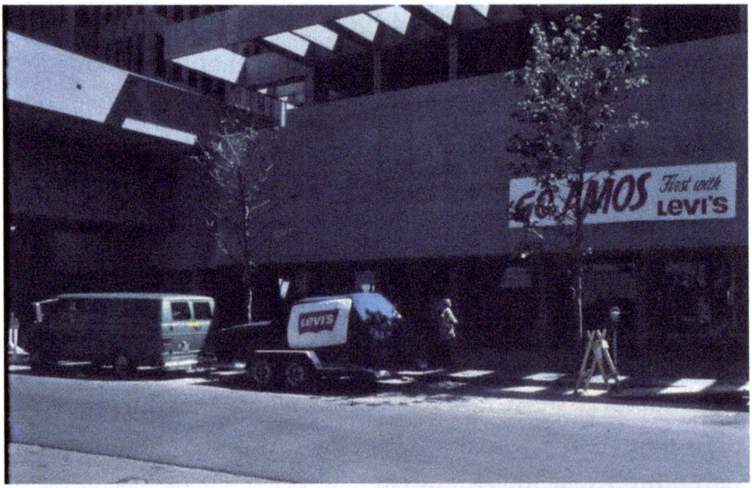
AMOS First with
LEVI'S
LEVI'S

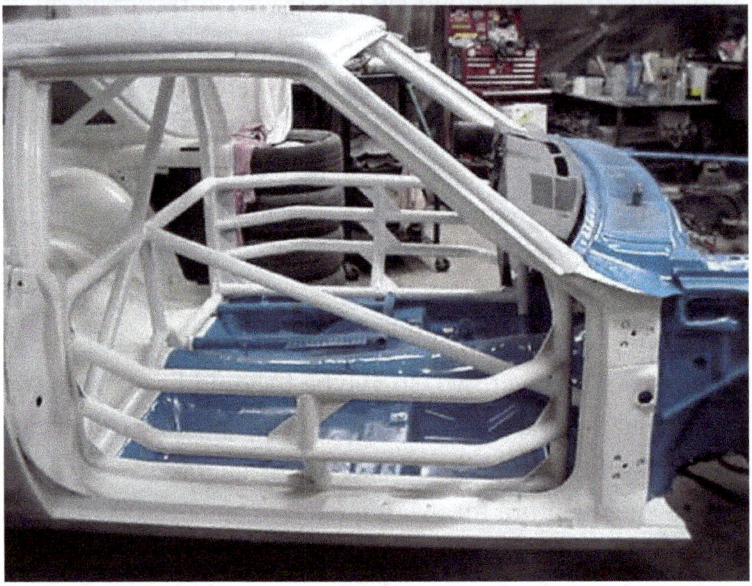

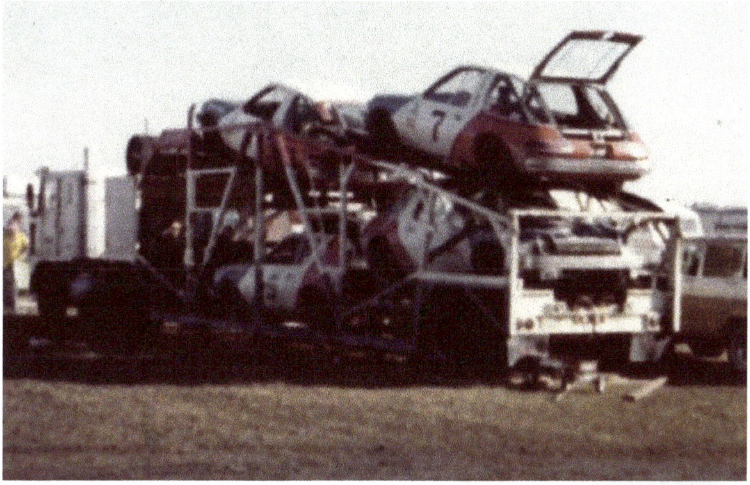

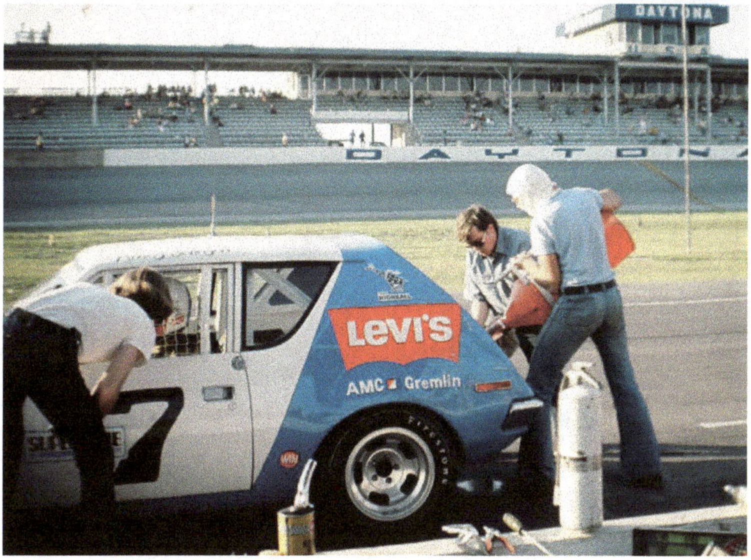
DAYTONA
DAYTONA
Levi's
AMC Gremlin

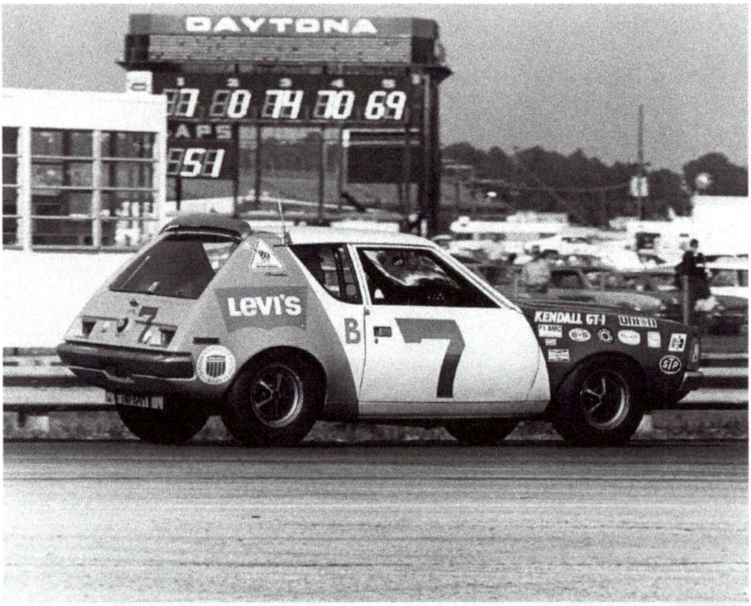
DAYTONA
Levi's
B
7
KENDALL GT-1
STP

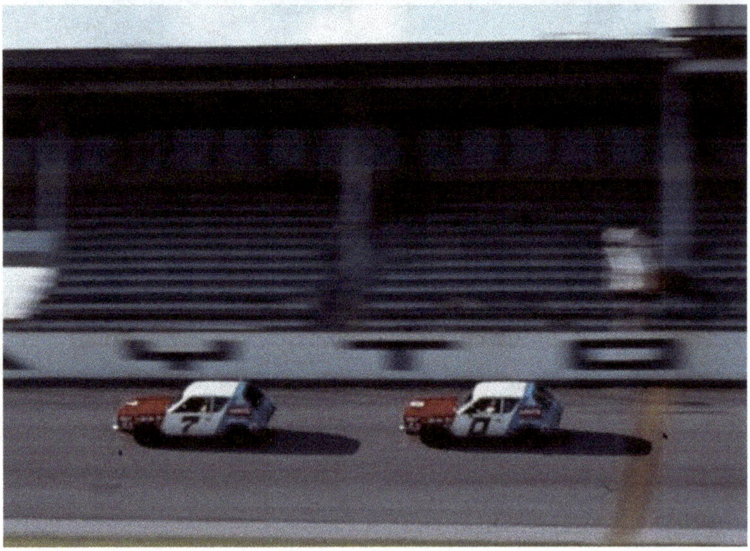
7

# 7
# AMC Pacer

Another one of AMC's rather unusual cars was the next one they wanted us to race. The Pacer was unique in that it had huge glass areas, and the right-side door was four inches longer than the left. My friend Joe Purcell took our first one West to Bill Ellis to have a cage welded in it and just dropped it at his place without any conversation. The next morning, I had a phone call from Bill: "Where the hell am I supposed to put the roll-hoop? The door opening on the right is bigger than the left". I told him to just split the difference. There were other things that were different about this car; it was wider, and the back of the engine was about 6 inches behind the front of the windshield. Originally, the Pacer was intended to have a smaller, rotary engine, but then they put the same old 232cid six-cylinder engine in it; however, it had a new 2-barrel carburetor for more power.

I had a talk with IMSA's technical director, Charlie Rainville, with whom I had made friends, and his decision was that it would be my choice: the old 1-barrel carb with the optional front disc brakes or the standard 2-barrel carb with the standard 4-wheel drum brakes. I would try the latter for my first race at the November Daytona finale. I would go faster on the straight but have trouble stopping the car at the end. It turned out to be a bad decision on my part, and I finished that race in seventh place. For the 1977 season, IMSA would add races, bringing the total to 15 races, and I would win one of them at the Talladega Speedway near the end of the season. By that time, we were racing two Pacers ourselves and renting two Gremlins and one more Pacer. The man renting the Pacer came to me complaining that his car was not the same as the one I was racing; so I drove his car in the next practice and turned the second fastest time of all cars. We always gave our customers the same that we had, and the cars we sold would have everything the same as our own cars. At an earlier race, someone came to me complaining about the carburetor he had bought from me. I gave him a wrench and told him to swap his carburetor for the one in my car, which he did. I would modify those Carter YF 1-barrel carbs three at a time and run each one on our dynamometer to check that they were the same.

The dynamometer we had had been a gift from my brother-in-law, Bill Watts, who was a big fan of racing. He was a champion amateur golfer who decided not to turn professional but to design and build golf courses. Several summers, between years in college, I had worked for him at the Florida courses he was constructing. He had even bought my first Austin Healey racecar when I moved on to the MGB. Bill had asked me one time why some people's cars were faster than the same model that others had. When I explained that a dynamometer was a piece of shop equipment that allowed you to run your engine in the shop and measure its horsepower, he said he would buy me one. That had given Team Highball an advantage over our competition. And I put a sponsor decal on our Gremlins: "Billy Watts, Golf Course Architect".

We would race our Pacers fifteen times in 1977 and fourteen times in 1978, Dennis getting two wins, and I got only one. The car was just too big and heavy. In 1978

IMSA had scheduled a GT race at Talladega, as its third race of the season, too close behind the Daytona and Sebring endurance races for many GT teams. As a result, they did not have a full field of cars and decided to let our RS cars enter that GT race in addition to our regular race. So, with my old friend Roger Mandeville as my co-driver and crew chief Jim Woodward as Dennis' co-driver, we entered our Pacers. My car won the class, and Dennis' car was second. Roger Mandeville was there that weekend because he was by then racing against us in the Goodrich Challenge RS series. My old Team Highball teammate, Paul Fleming, had bought and raced the first Mazda RX-2, a rotary-engine car in America, and then turned it over to Roger to race. I guess you could call us "friendly competitors." In the future, Roger and I would team up, and win many races.

It was in my Pacer that I had my most serious crash. At the end of the back straightaway, in a practice session at Mid-Ohio, my brake pedal went to the floor and stayed there. It is amazing how fast my mind went. There was a dirt bank beyond that turn at the end that had injured a few drivers and even killed one I had known, Patrick Jacquemart. So, I wanted to turn the Pacer around to hit the sand bank backward, letting my seat absorb the 100 mph plus impact. In the process, my tires would trip on the edge of the track, launching the car up and over. I hit backward and upside down and walked away with only some sand in my eyes. A couple of weeks later I would receive by mail a photo of my flying Pacer. The car was destroyed, but we had a spare, unsold Pacer with us for me to start the race in 51$^{st}$ place; I finished In 7$^{th}$. Dennis didn't like the engine in his car and had changed it for the one from my crash. He started from the pole position and won that race. The racing bucket seat that had saved me was one that we made for all our cars. We had a friend, Benton Stubbs, who worked in a Carolina boat building business, and he would, on his own, make the seats for us. Over the years, he must have made about fifty seats, one he had to re-make for an extra-wide co-driver of mine, Dick Barbour, and I would have to have removable padding when I was in the car.

We sold several of the Pacers, but we continued to support the Gremlins and even, on our own, ran a Gremlin successfully in the Daytona 24-hour race and the Sebring 12-hour where they had to race against V-8 powered cars and foreign sports cars. Just to finish one of the endurance races was considered a success, to win your class was over the top. We finally built an AMC Hornet hatchback with a 360 V-8 engine to be more competitive in the GT0 class and the Kelly AAC (All American) class of "Pony Cars." It was a success also. Once I bought an older one of the Hornets to be my street car. We had all the like-new interior from our stripped-out Gremlins, so it looked good. I liked the newest front bodywork of the 1975 Gremlin so much that I put it on my Hornet and gave it a nice white paint job. We had a race at Road Atlanta, and as Bunny and I pulled up to where all our cars were set up in the paddock, our AMC Competition Manager, Jim Rader, stepped out to greet us, and his mouth fell open. "Where did you get that?" After I told him I made it, he said that that was their next year's new AMC Concord model. But the next year, they would want us to race the new AMC Spirit in IMSA, and we were very much looking forward to being the first to race it.

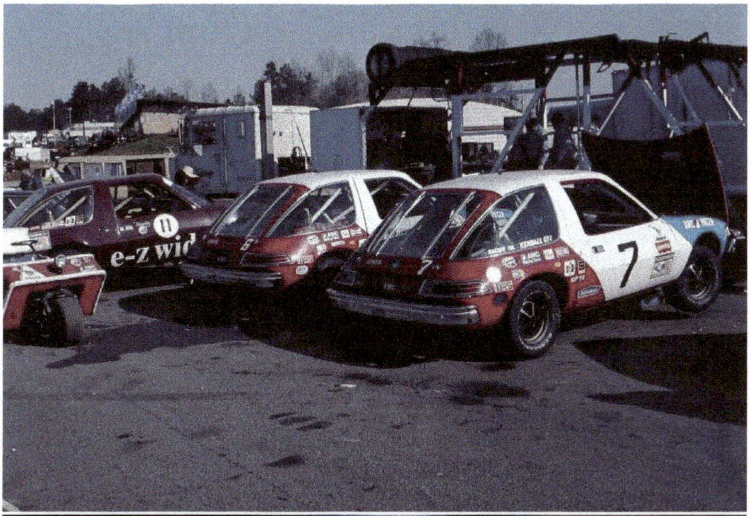
11
7

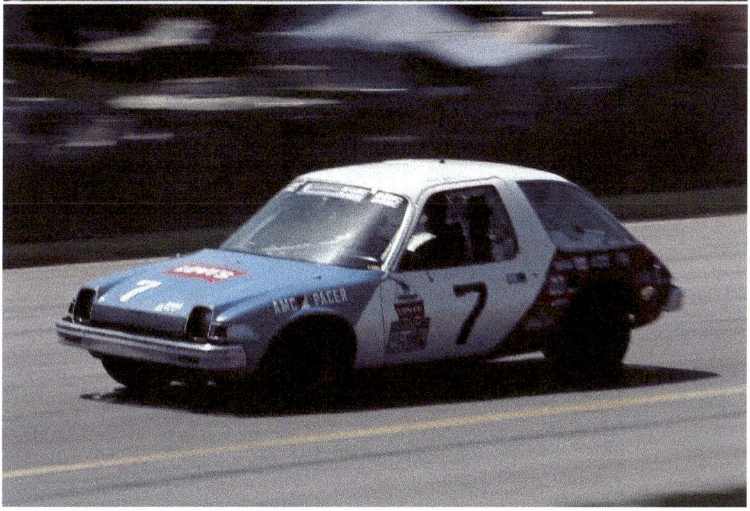
7
AMC PACER
7

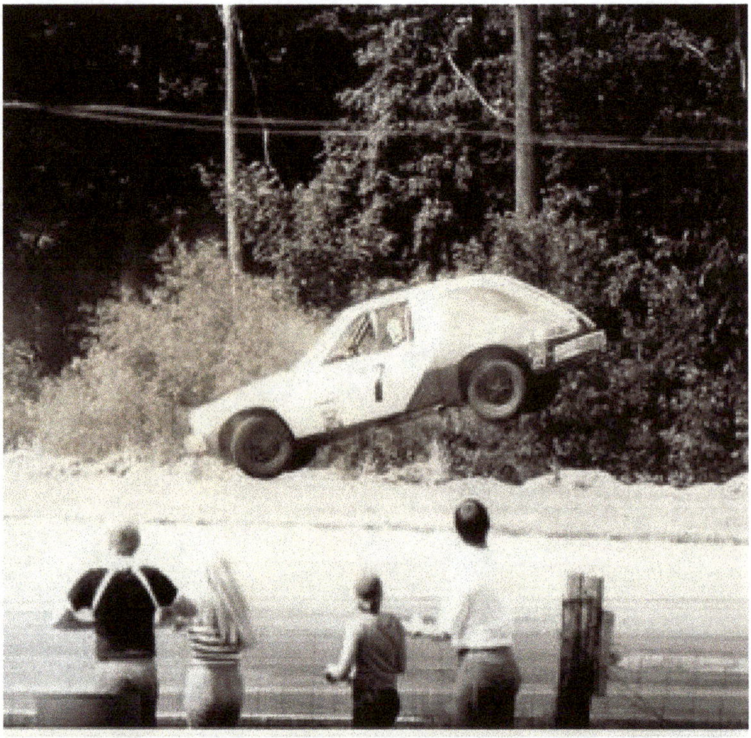

# 8
# AMC Spirit

I could hardly wait to get my hands on the new AMC Spirit. It came in only one body style, the two-door sedan, but that was an aerodynamic, slightly smaller version of a Chevrolet Camaro. The base model had our favorite six-cylinder engine that was so familiar to us, and it also came as a sporty Spirit AMX with a 304 cubic inch V-8 and some special body trim. We would be able to them race both in the next three years. The best change for our racing was that even the base model came with a 4-speed transmission, and we could leave the Gremlin's 3-speed gearbox behind. Since we were familiar with the suspension and running gear from our Gremlin days, it would be simple to get the first one on the track for the final IMSA race of 1978 at Daytona. That first race for the Spirit would see me finish sixth, right behind Dennis' Pacer, in the field of 51 RS cars. A pair of V-6 Buick Skyhawks and a pair of rotary-engine RX-2 Mazdas beat us to the checkered flag.

The first race of 1979 was back at Daytona where I opened the year with a victory in my AMC Spirit, and followed that at Sebring with a one-two, with Dennis on top. Roger Mandeville and Jim Downing showed a good start to their year in the new Mazda RX-3s. I would be a co-driver with them in a factory RX-7 GTX class car for the 12-hour endurance race at Sebring. This RX-7 was a new GTU class car that went too fast and finished too well at Daytona's 24-hour race (fifth over-all); so, IMSA had to reassess the rules for rotary engine cars and for the next race wanted Mazda to add four hundred pounds of ballast.

Damon Barnett said no; we would race in a different class, GTX and finish 6$^{th}$ in class. My long-time connection with Roger was beginning to pay off through his relationship with the Mazda factory and their American Competition Manager, Damon Barnett. In July of 1980, there was a special 6-hour RS race at Daytona where we would take FIA co-drivers that were earning points for an International Endurance Championship: Dennis, with Don Whittington, would win it, and I, with Dick Barbour, would finish fifth. There were 62 cars in that race. Dick Barbour had raced with us in one of the earlier FIA endurance races and was the reason we had put a "wide body" seat in my car. He was a car dealer from California who had a way of making things happen. For one LeMans 24-hour race he convinced Porsche he had a sponsor and Paul Newman as a driver; he convinced Newman he had cars and sponsors and convinced a good sponsor he had Porsche and Newman. That all worked, and he raced at LeMans, finishing fifth overall. He offered me the chance to run in the race in France, but I couldn't rationalize paying five thousand for one race. There are two ways to be a race driver: you can pay to race, or you can be paid to race.

    At one of the earlier race weekends in 1979, while at a dinner with my sponsors from BFG and AMC, I mentioned that I had learned of a 24-hour FIA race at the Nürburgring racetrack in Germany where the AMC Spirit AMX V-8 could race. Gary Pace (BFG) loved the Idea, and Jim Rader thought he might be able to interest AMC. Jim Rader was a fan of mine. Once, at Talladega, he had been refused entry to the NASCAR paddock where Roger Penske's AMC Matador was located. Our IMSA support racers were in a different paddock. When he told me what had happened, I took him back to the NASCAR gate, where we were stopped. I asked the man if he had communications with Bill Gazaway. He did, so I told him to tell Bill that Amos Johnson wanted to bring the AMC competition director in to see the Penske car. After that, a door opened, and Bill stuck his head out and waived us in. Point made! The tires for Nürburgring were restricted in size to 8 inches of tread width, and I thought we could get the Spirit accepted by the FIA. An American team from Chevrolet had tried once before but failed to finish the race. In a short time, I got the go-ahead from all. Gary got a budget from BFG, Jim got three cars from AMC, and I bought a couple more. We would continue with the IMSA RS races while the Team prepared three cars for the race. Team Highball would have to hire more mechanics and call on our local helpers. We had moved into a 5,000-square-foot shop the year before, and I had hired one of my after-hours helpers' wife for our front office and timing and scoring at the tracks, Lee and Ann Brantley. In December of 1977, Bunny and I had found time to slip off to my home area of Eastern North Carolina and get married in a small chapel built by my ancestors; for witnesses, we had my new three stepsons. She was still working for Dr Paul Fleming but would be helping at Team Highball.

  A friend of mine from England, Jeremy Nightengale, could help with the FIA approval by flying to the factory in Kenosha, Wisconsin, where I would meet him to fill out the FIA homologation papers for him to hand-carry to France. We had to have pictures and descriptions of all the parts we wanted to use on the car. It was good we got the car accepted; we had already begun preparing the cars. Again, we were familiar with everything about the car except the V-8 engine, but Dennis and I had rebuilt other V-8s before. We had one trick up our sleeve. One problem we had solved with our earlier endurance race V8 engines was maintaining good oil pressure without having a dry-sump oil pump. The answer was a simple, small container that could hold a couple of extra quarts of oil under pressure. Accusump was the name of the system we had found; it was mounted in the car where the driver could open a valve when cranking the engine and close it just before shutting the motor off. It saved the engine from losing oil pressure in hard cornering. The first two AMXs would be rushed through and shipped to England. One would be for the street to be a demonstration of this FIA accepted car, and the other was intended to be our first racing version. Jeremy would handle these. He was also connected to one of our long-time rental drivers, Les Delano, whose New York business also had offices in London. Bunny and I would fly over with one of our mechanics, Bill Brown, to race this first car at a 24-hour race at SPA/Francorchamps, Belgium. We made it there, ran practice and qualifying, but did not race. It was a fun trip for us and a good introduction to European racing; we stayed in a hotel near the track, working on the car in the basement of the hotel and driving the car on the street back and forth from the track. We had a sponsor from Brussels, Rick's Café American, that would bring us hot meals to the track. I had hoped to race on the old SPA course through the countryside but had to settle for their new Formula One track. A misunderstanding of the qualifying procedure kept us out of the race. I did not feel too badly about it because, frankly, the car and the team were not yet ready for a race. Les would go on to race in some of the shorter races in Europe, and Jeremy would bring our other AMX to meet us in Germany.

A BFG design team sent a drawing of the paint scheme we would have to use; they had bought a new Truck (transporter), and it would be painted to match. The whole rig with two race cars would be shipped over for the race along with equipment, spares, tires and our two friendly truck drivers, Frank and Buddy, who would also be our tire engineers. Each AMX would have three drivers for the race: Number "1" would be me, Dennis and James Brolin, the actor. Number "2" would have Jim Downing, Gary Witzenburg and Lyn St. James. Gary pace brought James Brolin into the group; AMC gave him a Jeep for participating. He turned out to be a good driver, an old California hotrodder. Jim Downing came replacing Roger Mandeville who had prior commitments. Gary Witzenburg was another BFG selection because he was not only a good driver but also a good writer and would put the story into several magazines. Gary Pace made the last pick, Lyn St. James, one of America's rising females of automobile racing who would go on to racing at the Indianapolis 500. By race time, we had a total of 36 in the cast, including the film crew that would be putting together a show for television and theaters. But the cars had a hard time getting through customs, and we wound up "bribing" the border agents with a big box of AMC red, white and blue winter racing jackets that had not been listed on the inventory.

We would be racing on the old circuit that was about nine miles long with over a hundred turns. The track was so big that there were three towns and Nurburg castle within the permanent racetrack. There were 113 cars in the race in five FIA classes; we would start 20$^{th}$ and 21$^{st}$ in the first wave of cars. Then, in turn, there would be two more waves starting before the leaders would finish the first lap. Most of the drivers had been racing here for years; we had not, but we had been there for a week, and the track had been open to anyone who would pay four marks per lap to practice. BFG set up an account for us to go out in pairs. We had a Mercedes, an Opal and our Spirit AMX that had been sent ahead. Goodrich paid for the six of us to have instruction from an older track champion. Brolin and I got the AMX for the practice. It was the only time I have ever started a race without being able to mentally drive a whole lap. I would start in #1; Downing would start in #2, 20$^{th}$ and 21$^{st}$ on the grid. My car was set up to go a little faster with different gearing and the other car was supposed to be a finisher for sure. As it turned out, both cars would finish. After my Spirit had a few extra problems, the #2 finished first, and our #1 came in second in class. We had part of our team with us on this trip, Bill Brown, Jim Woodward, Bill Cotton, Joe Lasher, Joe Purcell and Anne Brantley, for timing and scoring, and each of the drivers could bring along a significant other. We pretty much took over the Hotel Amring beside one of the straightaways. The week was a definite success. And you can find the film on You Tube: "Team Highball Nürburgring".

To finish the film, BFG's crew would need to do a bit more work back here. We rented a test track in

Savannah, GA, and I made a moving camera mount that fit in the trunk of a rental car. With two people also in the trunk, we got the shot they wanted: the camera started at ground level in front of the moving car, came up and zoomed in on the driver. I think they paid me $800 for the shot that would have cost them thousands of dollars if done in Hollywood. Another thing they needed was a video of Jim Brolin at the end of the race. He had been watching the last of the race from the roof of our Hotel Amring. So, Brolin and the car were at the 1980 Road Atlanta IMSA race, where we shot two scenes for the film. Jim set it up, having the two of us in our driving suits, messed up hair, and sweat (sprayed water) on our dirty faces, we raised our helmets and cheered our victory. That night we set the car up in the dark; with a hose spraying water on it while we rocked the car, headlights being interrupted by people running back and forth behind the car, Jim was at the wheel "racing in the rain". One more part of that scene would come when our cars were transported to California for a BFG poster shoot on Little Soggy dry lakebed near Ventura, CA. We would use a mountain road behind Brolin's home. They wanted a video of their tire running through rainwater. I made a mount for them that hung the camera down from the rear bumper behind the tire. A spinning Lexan disc would allow the camera to "see" the tread as it ran through the water, which was provided by a water tank pulled ahead of the car. It worked, pure Hollywood. But you will have to see the film on YouTube.

    Once back from Germany, we were able to finish out our 16 race IMSA season with Dennis just ahead of me, fourth in the points for the year. We built several of the

Spirit racecars for customers and rental rides. It was turning into a very successful racecar. For one buyer, Kal Showket, it was the second car purchased from Team Highball; he would buy a Mazda from us later and win an IMSA championship.

The 1980 season would be our last with the Levi's and American Motors sponsorships; Dennis and I would race that last year with our RS Spirits, starting with Daytona. The week before leaving for the February races I had a phone call from Mazda's Damon Barnett; their European driver, Tom Walkingshaw, had broken his leg while snow skiing. Would I be willing to take his place in the factory RX7 for the 24-hour race? I would co-drive with Australian driver Alan Moffat and Californian Stu Fisher, and I would still drive my Spirit in the RS race. That was a great way to start the year. The rotary engine RX7 was very fast, and by the $18^{th}$ hour we were an incredible first in our class and fifth place overall, and then our engine gave out. Even without running at the end of the race, we were listed $24^{th}$ out of 68. Roger Mandeville and Jim Downing finished $2^{nd}$ in class driving the other factory car. Four of us, Jim, Roger, Dennis and I, had finished in the top seven, racing against each other the day before in the BFG RS race. Irv Hoerr had won in a Spirit. We would spend the whole season racing each other. For the upcoming Sebring 12-hour race Dennis and I would be in a V-8 Spirit AMX with Lou Statzer, sponsored by his Caribbean AMC/Jeep dealership, and Dennis and I would also be in the RS preliminary race. However, the day of the 12-hour race, Downing was unwell, and they asked me to take his seat in the RX7. That year, we won the GTU class.

Dennis and Lou had problems and did not finish with the V-8 AMX. In the preliminary, Downing's RX3 won, and my Spirit was 4$^{th}$.

The remainder of the 1980 season I raced 12 more RS class races with three 2$^{nd}$ place finishes; Dennis got one RS victory at Elkhart Lake, Wisconsin, where I finished 3$^{rd}$ in the Kelly American Challenge with the V-8 Spirit AMX. Charlie Rainville, IMSA's Technical Director, and my friend had called me to say that they needed my car for the Kelly race. When I told him my engine was oversized for the Kelly AC rules, he said for me to bring the car, but don't finish higher than third, and they would not check my car after the race. During that race, several of the regular drivers crashed, and I wound up third. That was the only time I ever raced a knowingly illegal car in IMSA. I swear! But I had permission. I ran five of those races, in Legal cars, looking for new venues for Team Highball for the next year. We built one lighter weight Spirit for the Kelly series with our 232cid six cylinder. The only difference in the engine was triple, side draft carburetors replacing the one-barrel Carter; that was a huge gain in power. I enjoyed driving that car against the heavy V8 cars, and we wound up letting Cat Kiser have it for the series. She was an SCCA champion, and women drivers got bonus prize money in the Kelly Girl Challenge series. I also put Cathy Rude in one of the V8 Spirits for a few races.

I did have one drive lined up for '81, though. B. F. Goodrich would sponsor Roger Mandeville's GTU class Mazda RX7 in the Camel GT series, and I would be his co-driver.

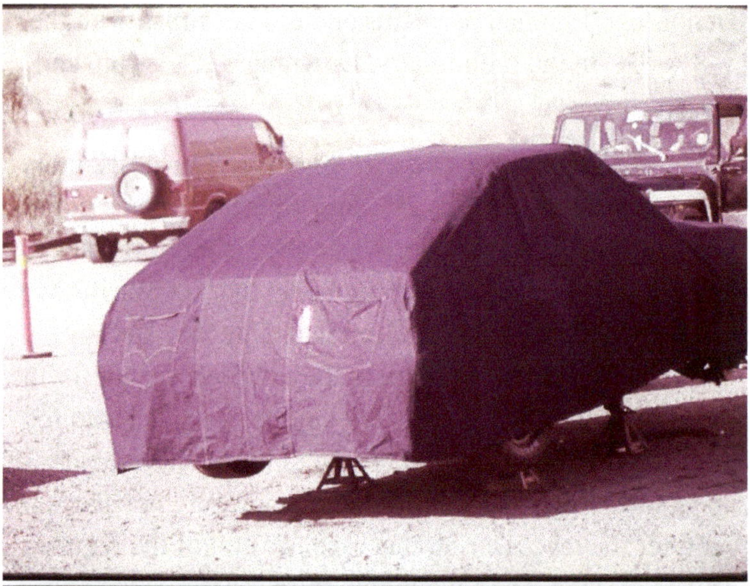

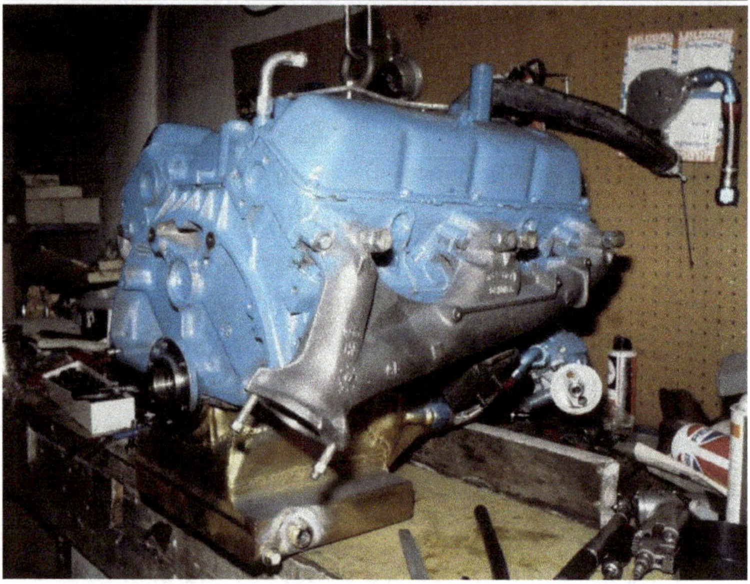

BFGoodrich
T/A
Performance Tires
T/A
Performance Tires
BFGoodrich

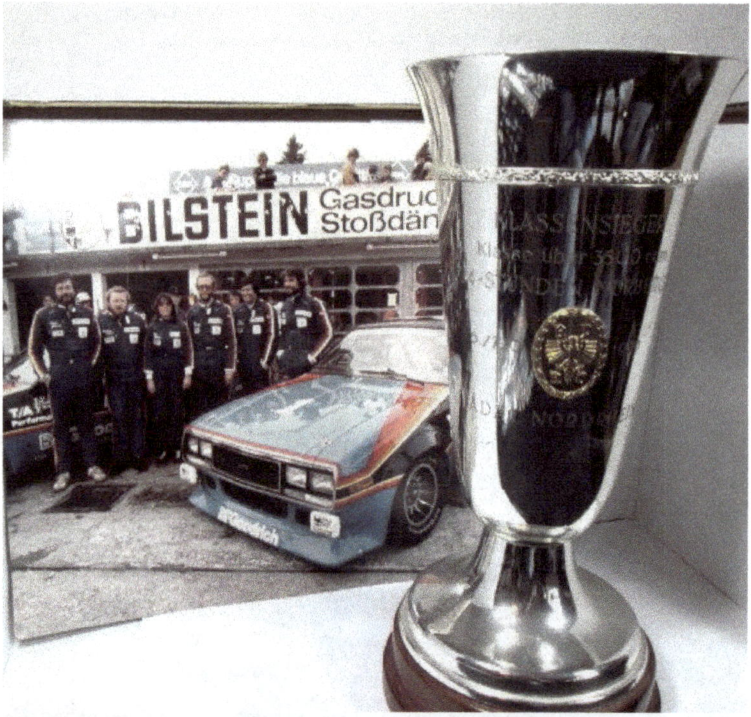
BILSTEIN

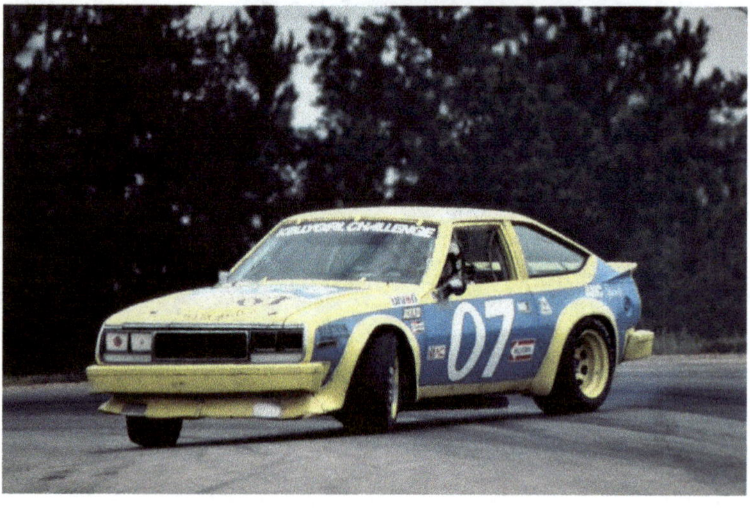
07

# 9
# Mazda Sedans

Mazda Motors would be my main sponsor for the 1981 season, not as a car builder, but only as a driver. On my own I would continue to race my remaining AMCs in events that were convenient. Team Highball was in the process of selling our AMC cars, and Dennis would stay with us, continuing to build engines. There would be eight Camel GT endurance races for me in Roger's BFG sponsored RX7, beginning with Daytona and Sebring. I would run in nine of the RS races, eight with my Spirit and one with Roger, in his Mazda RX3, that was a 6-hour at Daytona which we won. I also raced four times in the Kelly AC series with the AMX. My farewell race for American Motors, after ten years, came at Daytona, where my Spirit ran faster than ever (about 150mph) and shredded a tire while leading the race, finishing eighth.

I had done a good job as a driver for Mazda; so, beginning in1982 Damon Barnett would keep me as Roger's co-driver and give me a contract to build and race their piston-engine, front wheel drive GLC in IMSAs newly named International Sedan (IS) class races. I would race in Roger's RX7 eight times, with three victories coming at the Sebring 12, Road Atlanta and Mosport, Canada, which had been Roger's home track before moving to the U.S.

Mazda had only raced their rotary engines, and it would be a first for them when I ran my 4-cylinder GLC in its first race at Road Atlanta in April of '82. We had been given a car with slight hail damage for a starter. With time short, we did what we could by stripping out the car for a cage and one of our bucket seats, widened the stock steel wheels and did some port work on the engine. Lunoti Camshafts ground us one by first welding up the lobes and then regrinding them for racing, and I welded an exhaust header for the car and used exhaust tubing to make my own intake manifold for the mandatory Holly two-barrel carburetor. We were able to run the engine briefly on our dyno (175 hp) before loading up and heading to Atlanta for its first race. We had no spares for the GLC but made the race, and, at the end of it, I had finished an amazing first in the IS class and second overall, only 13 seconds behind Jim Downing's winning RS Mazda RX3. That result definitely got the factory's attention; they invited me for a visit to the Factory in Japan at the end of the year. and please, Mr. Johnson, bring camshaft, exhaust header, Carburetor and intake manifold for our engineers to see. That would be one of my four trips to Japan, three of which included my wife, Bunny. There would be a total of 14 races for the GLC, but no more wins.

 A "one-off" drive I had that year came in a Renault Cup race at Road Atlanta. Bunny, Steve Coleman and I helped IMSA start a new series for that year for Renault R5 cars. The cars were all identically prepared using a performance kit supplied by the factory. It was such a good idea that cars were still being set up in the paddock the day before the first race at Road Atlanta. We had produced over 40 racecars; one was for me. I managed to win pole position in qualifying and was up front for a few laps until running out of gas. The gas gauge was defective, and none of the crew added gas. I sold my car, but Dennis went on to win at Atlanta and finish in the top three for the year, thus earning a trip to France to race against European racers. IMSA would run that class of races for the next four years, but Dennis would be back in a second Team Highball Mazda GLC the next year. Another interesting connection to Renault came when I got a call from Patrick Jacquemart, a French driver representing the Renault racing team that was coming into IMSA with an IS front wheel drive R-5 racecar. He was such a gentleman that he was asking my permission to approach my crew chief, Jim Woodward, with an offer of a job with Renault. For Jim's sake, I could not say no. Later, in practice before a race at Road Atlanta, Jim would ask me to drive their Renault a few laps to help with a problem they were having.

There would be 14 GTU races with Roger in 1983, with four wins starting at Brainard, Minnesota, and then three in a row, Portland, Oregon, Mosport, Canada and Elkhart Lake, Wisconsin. Then he would win a couple of more short races, driving alone to lock up the GTU championship. In June of that year, Damon would have the two of us race a different GLC that he gave us in an SCCA 24-hour race called The Longest Day of Nelson Ledges in Ohio. It was a fun race, with an extra driver, Rod Millan, Australian driver of rally fame, and Damon came along as Manager and cook. We finished $2^{nd}$ in our class. At Portland that year, we had a newly built extra GLC with us, and I told Kal Showket I had built it for him. He said he would stay with his new Ford Escort; so I asked Roger to drive it in the race, where Roger beat Kal. At the next race, Mid-Ohio, Kal said not to let Roger drive it again and he would take the car home after the race, and he did and won several races with it later. I would race my GLC 14 times in '83, with one victory at Sebring in a preliminary to the 12-hour race. We would get a second team car on the track for Dennis at the Daytona final race of the year. We would race the two GLCs at all 16 races in 1984 but were unable to get a victory against Tommy and Bobby Archer in their Renaults. They were ice racers from Minnesota, and driving the front wheel drive racecars is very much like driving on ice, a lot of side-ways sliding around but on dry pavement. The four races they did not win were won by the larger Dodge Daytonas. Before the next year I would spend a lot of hours after winter snowstorms playing with my street GLC on large, iced-over parking lots, and we would make some improvements on our cars. We had someone make gears for our transmissions that would allow us to change the individual gear ratios, making them fit the different tracks better. We would log track information for every track; so the next time there, the car would be better set up.

  Roger would build a new RX7 for 1984 with the larger 13B rotary engine, moving him up into the Camel GTO class against Camaros, Mustangs and the Nissan 300Z. We had a great year, winning at Riverside, CA together, and Roger won at Lime Rock, CT, alone. In the 14 races we were consistently finishing well enough for him to win the championship, and I wound up third place for that year. When Roger's RX7 had problems early in the GT race at Charlotte, NC, since I had not yet driven, Corvette driver Phil Currin's crew "drafted" me to be his co-driver. Once in his car, I wound up running first place in GTO until I was wrecked by a Porsche driver's mistake. The car was badly damaged, and I felt bad. But the car's owner turned out to be my old customer, Kal Showket, and he convinced me it was not a problem.

    With the GLCs, Dennis and I would run all 16 races in '84 without a win, but we were always competitive with the front runners, and we had built and sold a lot of cars. Bunny and I had a lot of fun when we raced the GLC at Detroit as a preliminary race to the Formula One U. S. Grand Prix. Damon's lady friend, Peg Gilman, was the chief registrar there and had the two of us be her assistants. We would go into the racing paddock to register all the members of the F-1 teams. I would come off the track from practice, change out of my driving suit and go into the restricted F-1 area to sign in the FIA teams. Ferrari's Niki Lauda tried to get us to give him a couple of extra passes for his lady friends. When we were returning to Peg's office, security stopped us, saying we had the wrong credentials. I opened the box I was carrying and asked which one I should be wearing. He laughed and said go on through. I had to learn how to ask them to sign the release in a couple of different languages; it was fun. Dennis was third, and I was fifth in our race. Team Highball had grown into a complete racing business. We were incorporated with me as president. The front office was Bunny with an assistant, Melanie Mann, Becky Bell as team manager, and a public relations manager, my stepson, Mike Diggett. In the shop, we had welders, painters, machinists and mechanics: Norm Samuelson, Bob Hubbard, Dan Robson, Terry Drum, Bill cotton, Danny Upchurch, Marshall McLeod, Rick Thompson, Rod Whaley, Quinton Brantley,

Louis Curcio, Whit Diggett (stepson), Dennis and me. And we were adding a street shop with a partner, Grover McNair. It turned out we were also a family business: Melanie Mann married Mike "Corky" Diggett, and Becky Bell was married to Norm Samuelson. Terry Drum married Bunny's sister, Jamie Dixon. Bunny and I had married in 1977, and two of her sons, Whit and Corky, worked at the shop; her third son, Tad Diggett, worked with us at the races.

IMSA had renamed our car class and eliminated rear-drive cars for 1985; we were now "Pro-Formance" sedans of the Goodrich Radial Challenge series. The Archer brothers Renaults were gone, also, as they had new contracts with Chevrolet. Dennis and I would start the year with the GLCs, and I would then have a new Mazda 626 later that year. I would miss two of the 14 races when I crashed the 626 badly at Riverside, CA. However, I would win two races: Lime Rock, Connecticut, with the GLC and Pocono, Pennsylvania, with the 626. Dennis would have a great year, winning four races and the championship for '85. I would be third for that year.

There were only 11 races in 1986, and I would win one in the 626 at Riverside, with Dennis's GLC taking second. I had a bad crash there the year before, cracking my sternum when I hit a concrete wall at speed. Dennis would get his only win for the year at Mid-Ohio, with me in third place. The following year would be about the same, only 11 races as IMSA continued to build their other racing series. I would win a thriller by inches at Elkhart Lake, Wisconsin, over the "new kid on the block", Parker Johnstone, in an Acura. With a win at Portland and four second places,

Dennis would take his new Mazda 323 to second for 1987 behind the Acura, and I would be fourth. The venerable GLC had seen its last, and it had been a "<u>G</u>ood <u>L</u>ittle <u>C</u>ar", but it was time to move on.

For the ten-race series of 1988, both Dennis and I would be in the improved Mazda 323, and I would get two victories, Road Atlanta and Lime Rock, and four runners-up for the year's second place behind Parker Johnstone. Dennis had no wins and a fourth place for the year. 1989 would be another 10-race year for our piston-powered Team Highball Mazda, but we would be in their new Turbocharged MX6, and for the third year in a row, there would be no race at Daytona for this series. I would manage a win at Lime Rock in the rain and be on the podium four more times on the way to fifth for the year, just behind the winless Dennis, who was fourth. The handwriting was on the wall. Damon Barnet had retired as Competition Manager, being replaced by Dick St. Ives, and he had different plans for Mazda's IMSA racing. Damon had, over the years, made Mazda the success that it was. He had a Japanese counterpart, Akio Kinoshita, and together, they had spread Mazda's budget over many teams, resulting in winning IMSA Manufacturer's Championships for many years in many classes. On any weekend, there were more Mazdas on racetracks than any other brand. Team Highball's contract was called off after the first three races of 1990. Team Highball had been selling cars and parts for these racing sedans for eight years, and since we had been selling some of them to South and Central America, the parts and engine sales would continue for a few more years. One morning, back then, I had a phone call, and a small voice said: "The men from Columbia are here". I drove the 5 miles to the Raleigh Durham airport, picked up two men and an eight-year-old kid, bringing them back to the shop. The boy was their interpreter, as the men spoke only Spanish. As they began looking at the 323 racecar, conversing in Spanish, I started answering them without going through the boy. So, if I understood their language, they had to be careful what they were saying. I had studied five years of Spanish in school; it would come in handy the rest of my life. We sold the car to Columbia, where they continued to race it for several more years.

-Chuck Ritz-

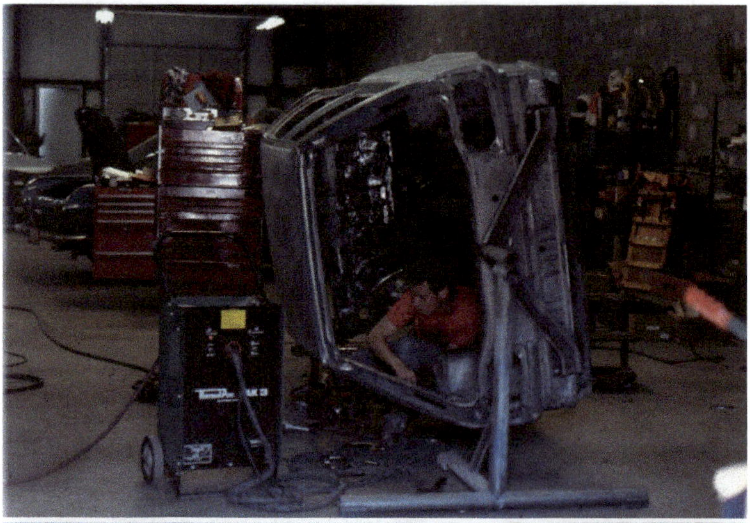

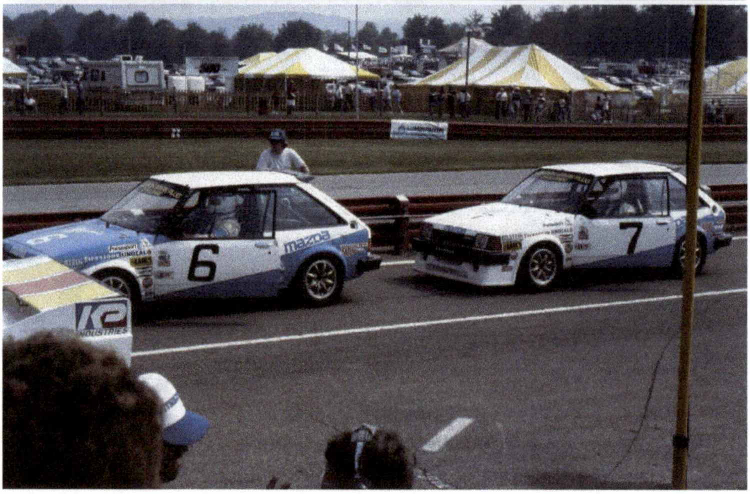
6
mazda
7

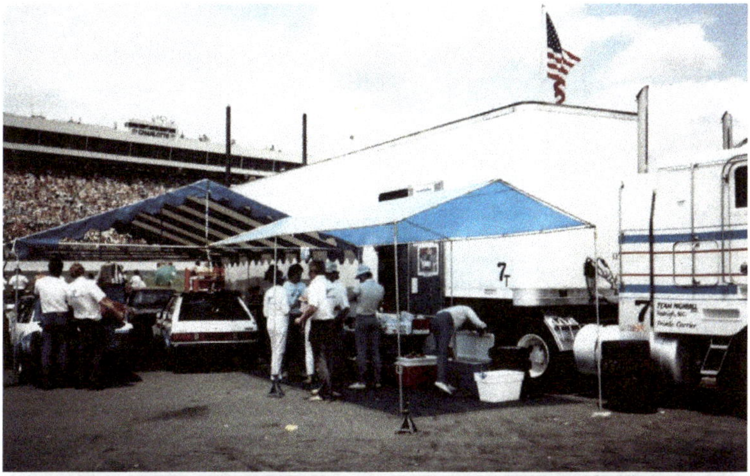

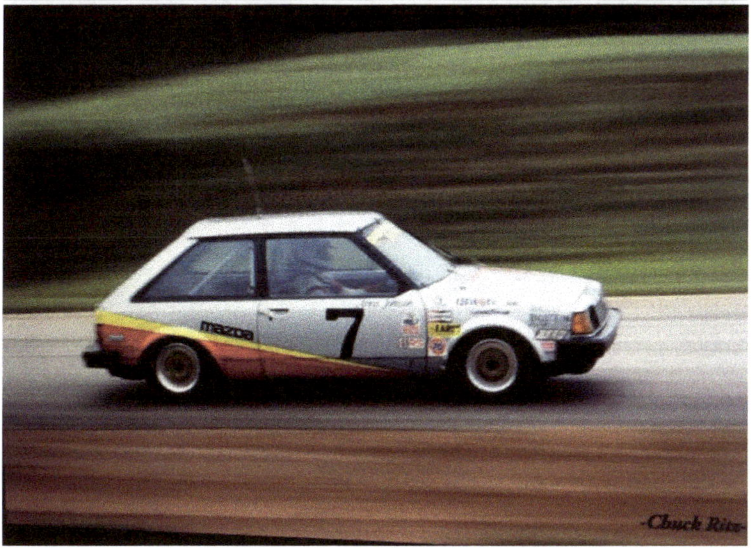
7
mazda
-Chuck Ritz-

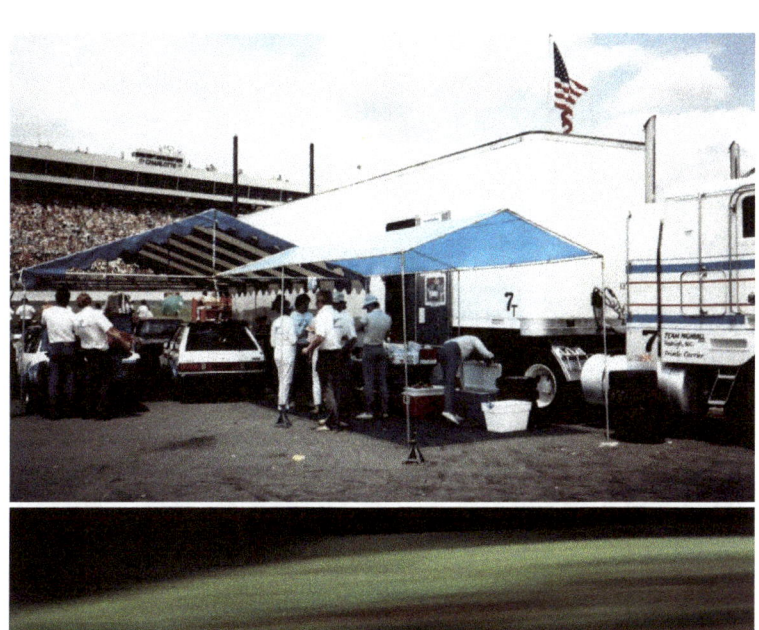

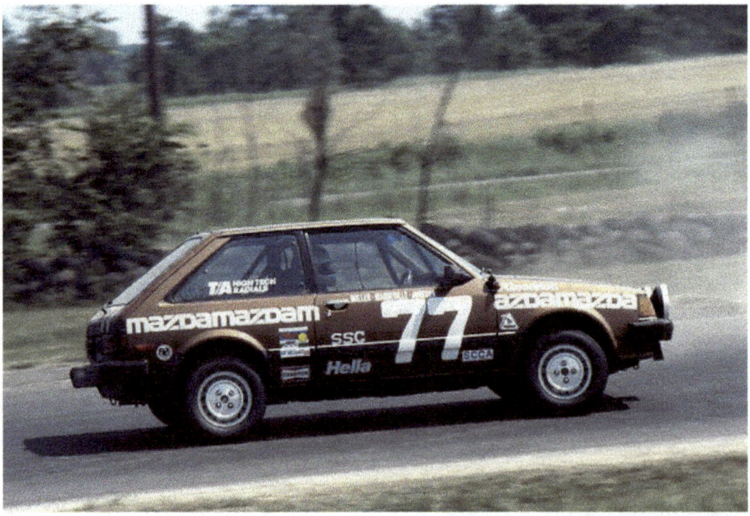
mazdamazdam
azdamazda
77
SSC
Hella
SCCA

# 10
# Mazda RX7

Team Highball's 1985 season started with a huge win in GTU at the Daytona 24-hour race. It is not an inexpensive thing to run these endurance races; at least five sets of tires would cost you more than $5,000 back then; however, Yokohama tires had been provided for Roger when I was his co-driver, and they would continue to sponsor my RX7. They also handled the service and technicians. There were times when Yokohama would fly tires in from Japan just for my cars and even put tires on my transporter. For this first Daytona race, the $20,000 prize and contingency money was a nice start to our year. It was a habit of mine to bonus the paid crew with prize money, so they loved winning. In the 17 races of the season, I was on the GTU podium 7 times, enough points to be third for the season and help Mazda win the manufacturer's championship. Unfortunately, my good friend Charlie Rainville, IMSA's Technical Director, passed away in 1984. To replace him, I was surprised to see that they had hired my old crew chief, Jim Woodward. I was still connected to the technical department.

The '86 season was a virtual repeat of the year before; 17 races, and we won the Daytona 24-hour with co-drivers Jack Dunham and, this time, my teammate, Dennis Shaw. Again, it would be my only win in GTU, third place for the year behind Tom Kendall and Roger Mandeville, both driving RX7s. Roger had been put back in GTU to ensure that we would get the Manufacturers Championship again. Team Highball, Inc. had become quite a team in IMSA racing; we had, in addition to employees, people who would come to the races year after year just to help. All we had to do was give them a pit pass and feed them at the track. Bill Humphries and Marty Parchuck would be there for all our Daytona races. They had their jobs and did them well. As for feeding them, we also fed sponsors, photographers and press people. Corky and Melanie, with help from Bunny and Becky and sometimes my mom, would set up a hospitality tent for anyone who needed a good sandwich. They even fed Gene Hackman's son, who was a vegetarian, when Damon brought him over.

By now, IMSA racing had fallen into a pattern, Florida's Daytona 24 and Sebring 12 endurance races would start the season in February and March, with maybe a street race at Miami. Next, we would go to the West Coast for two consecutive races, one at Riverside or Ontario and then Laguna Seca, near Monterey, or Sears Point, near San Francisco in California. By then, the country had warmed up enough that we could have our races at Road Atlanta, Mid-Ohio and maybe Watkins Glen, New York. Team Highball loved Road Atlanta; it was the closest IMSA track to home. We tire-tested there and took everything on wheels there for the races. We almost always would be at Lime Rock on Memorial Day, racing on a Monday because Connecticut would not permit racing on a Sunday. Some of us called it "Slime Rock" for all the times it would rain there. Next, we would make another two-race trip to the Northern part of the West Coast, Portland, Oregon's Rose Park track, in sight of Mount St. Helens and another Northern California track. Yes, we were out there for an earthquake and saw the results of the volcano eruption. IMSA would have races at Pocono, PA or Charlotte, NC, on its way back to finish the year at Daytona on Thanksgiving, where, most years, we had our celebratory annual banquet. That would give us December and January to recover and prepare for the next year. Sometime here I was approached by a Dr. Deborah Graham of International Sports Consultants who was working on a project to find out what characteristics made championship drivers, and I was one of those selected. I guess they wanted to know what made me "tick". Along with others, Pete Halsmer being one I knew, she asked me to fill out forms and questionnaires. A few months after I did that, I got a brief result and an offer of more complete information, for a fee. I didn't go for the extra, but this is what she said of me: Passive, Careful, Thoughtful, Peaceful, Controlled, Reliable, Even Tempered and Calm. All of that was in the Phlegmatic quadrant of results. I looked up the definition and, I guess, I'm OK with that.

I had made a habit of going to Vail, Colorado, for snow skiing before Christmas. Mark Yeager, one of our friendly race photographers, had made friends with a past Indianapolis racer, Bob Lazier, who owned a ski lodge there. About the first week of December, Bob would give big discounts to any of the racing community that wanted to come skiing at Vail. Bunny and I would take him up on the deal for nine years in a row. Yeager, friends Ed Jacobs and Dr. Al Bacon, Mazda racer from Tennessee, and a few others would join us there. We were a wild bunch on the mountain. Bob Lazier had his racing history and his Colorado history. A much younger and poorer Bob and his wife were towing a racecar to races in California when their car died on Vail Mountain. They both took jobs in the area to pay for repairs, but they would never leave. He and his family wound up owning two lodges and an arcade there. His two sons would both race in the Indianapolis 500, and son, Buddy Lazier, would win it one year. I made great friends with Bob and asked him to come out of retirement to co-drive with Dennis and me at the 1987 Daytona 24-hour race, and we would win it for the third year in a row. To race with us, he said all he wanted was peanut butter and diet Pepsi.

So, 1987 was a great year. In GTU, the re-bodied RX7 won Daytona to start and then won the Riverside 6-hour. Bob Lazier, Dennis Shaw, and I would take that first race of the season with a record finish. We had always approached the endurance races differently from sprint races. You should not race the other cars; you race against the track, protecting the car because it must last the whole race. Take no chances; do not draft other cars to go faster, and look in the mirrors so you don't get in the way of faster cars. Three drivers drive at a comfortable, fast pace, and we try to, all three, by using the same lines through the turns. If the cars that are passing you always know what you will be doing, you won't be caught up in a crash. If it is a race where you are the fastest class, there is a different plan. It worked for us before; however, this race was different. I was always the first driver, being able to stay out of trouble when so many cars were together trying to go fast. As it turned out two other RX7s wanted to stick with me, and we were at the front of the GTU class. I kept the speed up, and they stayed with me. The three of us were actually racing! After using a full tank of gas, each of us turned our cars over to co-drivers, who continued to race together. Then, one car had a problem, leaving two of us together, and hours later, the second car broke, leaving us with a huge lead over the Porsches and Nissans. We won our class over the next RX7 by 22 laps; in third was a Porsche driven by a good friend, Peter Uria. A strange thing happened Sunday morning during the race. Someone showed up from a restaurant in town with a full, warm breakfast, saying it had been ordered the day before to be delivered to the pits of the number 95 Leitzinger Nissan. Their instructions were to give it to Team Highball number 71 if the Nissan car was no longer in the race. Thank you, Bob Leitzinger; it was a very nice gesture. We had proved the durability of this well-built car, and my friend Bob Lazier was very happy with his gold medallion. Bunny and I were welcome anytime at his Tivoli Lodge after that win.

During the year, we built a copy of our RX7 for a customer in Puerto Rico, Juan Carlos (J.C.) Negron. He was married to an employee of American Airlines and could fly, direct into Raleigh Durham airport for free; so, as we completed parts for his car, he would come up to get them and carry them back home without a shipping fee. There were a few things that had to be shipped, like engine, transmission, rear-end, and, oh yes, the chassis, which we built on our "jig" and then cut in half to be used as a shipping crate for the bodywork. Once he had everything he needed, his team in Puerto Rico assembled the car. It was a unique "kit car". J.C. would come up to run a few races with us and even ship his car up for a couple of races in Florida. During the balance of the year, I added a victory at Summit Point in West Virginia and another at Watkins

Glen, NY. For the year, it would be a second-place behind Tom Kendall, driving Clayton Cunningham's West Coast Mazda RX7. I also picked up a win with the Mazda 626 ProFormance car at Elkhart Lake. And just for fun, I ran nine races in the new IMSA Firestone Firehawk series that ran improved street cars as a preliminary event for our other races. Damon had sold me a crashed RX7 for $100 which I repaired and could carry along in our transporter. My co-driver, Frank Folino, and I got on the podium twice, with a second and a third. Frank was one of our GLC customers from earlier, and together, we placed tenth in the Firehawk series for the year. The '87 season was the first time IMSA didn't end up at Daytona; Del Mar, near San Diego, would be our last race, and Bunny and I would then take a week off in Ensenada, Mexico.

No one had ever done it; I would be the first to win four Daytona 24-hour class races in a row, all four in the same car. This time with Dennis and Bob helping again. Bob was dyslexic, as was his son Buddy; so I made some modifications to the car's dash gauges by putting a small piece of red tape at the maximum reading and a piece of blue tape at the minimum on each gauge. The gauges were rotated in the dash so that the optimum reading was directly vertical. We could glance at the dash and immediately see if anything was wrong. That worked so well that for the rest of my racing, my cars would have the same convenience. At the finish, my old Number 71 RX7 led a Mazda parade across the finish line, Roger's GTO RX7 and two other GTUs, an RX7 and Peter Uria's GTU Porsche 911, in third again. We won the class by 12 laps. I would be second for the year and on the podium four times with two wins and two second place finishes. And I was awarded a special Norelco cup for my drive to second place at Elkhart Lake that year.

During a break in IMSA's schedule, I accepted an offer to drive in an SCCA Trans Am race in the streets of Niagara Falls, New York. They wanted to know how their cars compared to the IMSA cars and had invited Roger Mandeville to bring his three-rotor GTO RX7 to that race. There was a local racer, David Yarmoluk, who had a two-rotor SCCA RX7 that would also be in the race; I would be his co-driver. David's car builder was Bob Cuneo, the man that would later build all the MX6s except mine. In that race, co-drivers were not mandatory; so the plan was for me to qualify the car and start the race with David taking over at the refueling stop mid-race. The track was short, and the pavement was slick, with the heavier V-8 and V-6 Mustangs, Camaros and Corvettes struggling to go fast and the two Audi 4-wheel drive cars and me enjoying the race. I started mid-pack in the field of over 30 cars, and by pitstop time, I was eighth. David said for me to stay in the car, and I finished sixth overall, just ahead of Roger and Lyn St. James. Bob and David were so amazed and happy with that result that they gave me $5,000 from the prize money.

Our old "war horse" was struggling in the shorter races, and there were more of them now, with only 12 races for the season. It was time to build a new, updated car; taking advantage of the rules would be the way to a faster car. We gave it a new five-speed transmission and independent rear suspension, still utilizing the same differential and gears from Franklin Engineering. For the engine, we got a new electronic fuel injection and a lighter carbon fiber clutch on an aluminum flywheel. The ignition system was one I came up with where each of the two rotors was treated as a separate one rotor engine, running at half the speed. The MSD (multiple spark discharge) people told me that their system only made extra power below 5,000 rpm, and my separated engine accepted that it was only running at half speed when it was at 9,000. On our dyno, we saw a gain of about 10 hp.Everyone took care to save weight wherever we could. If the car came in too light, we could add ballast where it could balance the car better. The new RX7 would be ready for the last two races of the year, and I would let Dennis do the break-in at a street race in Columbus, Ohio. I would finish fourth, and Dennis would be nineth in the new car. I'm sure he was being careful with it. Roger Mandeville had to send his GTO RX7 to Japan before the last race at Del Mar, California and came to me with a request. Our sponsor, Yokohama, would ask me to paint my new car like his and run his usual number, 38, to complete the annual sponsorship. I would drive the yellow number 38, and Roger would drive my blue and white number 71 in that last 45-minute sprint race. Nancy Mandeville had always done the lap times for Roger, and Bunny would keep mine. They were both long-time timing and scoring "Pros". They found it so difficult to hit the stopwatch on the correct car at Del Mar that they decided to swap husbands for the weekend. My new car had been the lightest car we had built, light enough to go back to a smaller 12A rotary engine for acceleration on this short course set up in the parking lot of a horse racing track. Ordinarily, I would use the larger13B for top speed on a long straightaway, but I had learned something from that SCCA Trans Am race earlier in the year. I would have my team set my changeable transmission gears so I could use all five gears on the track in the race. Usually, first gear was just for getting started out of the pits. For 45 minutes, I would be shifting like a madman.

I started the race from seventh place and rather quickly climbed up to the top three. By the halfway point, I had reached first, passing Tom Kendall's pole sitting Chevrolet Beretta. My plan was working. I would accelerate faster out of the turns, go deeper into the corners on braking and then his heavier car would catch me by the end of the short straights. On the last lap, just before the last turn, he reached my back bumper, and I was sent into the wall, spinning back across the track while the third placed car went over my car. My race was over; my car was destroyed. I climbed out to see it sitting on its belly-pan with no wheels. The rescue crew and TV announcers were surprised to see Amos, not Roger, climbing out of the wreck. Roger, in old number 71, had failed to finish the race. The race was over, and I was unhurt but mad. Back in the paddock, Dick St. Ives and the west coast Mazda people were sad but excited to have watched that race. Dick told me that he had about $60,000 left in his budget for the year and would send it to me to rebuild the car. But, for next year, he wanted it rebodied as a GTU MX6. It would be the first MX6, replacing the old, very successful RX7. After that, Corky, Mel, Bunny, and I needed another week-long trip to Ensenada

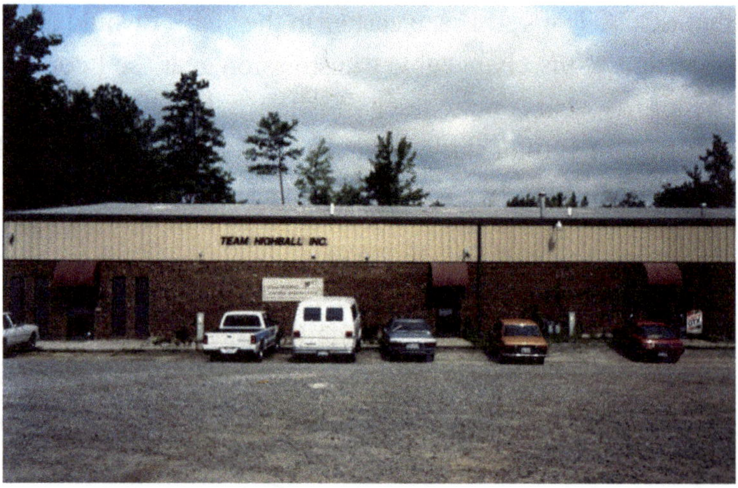
TEAM HIGHBALL INC.

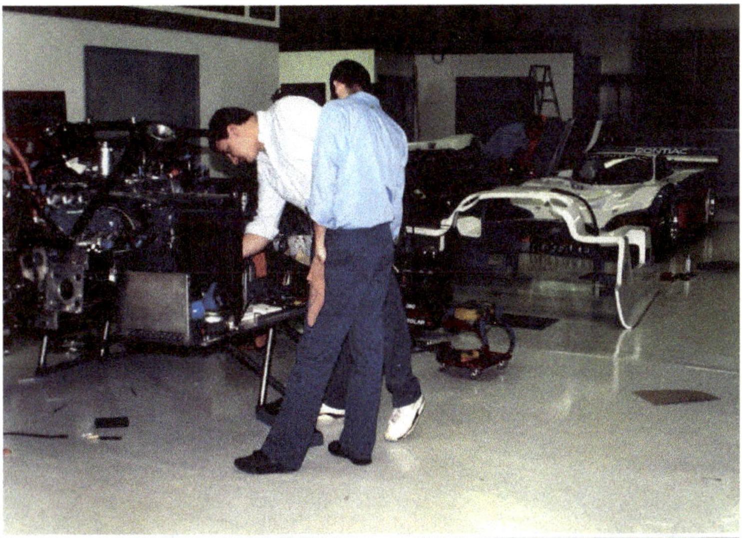

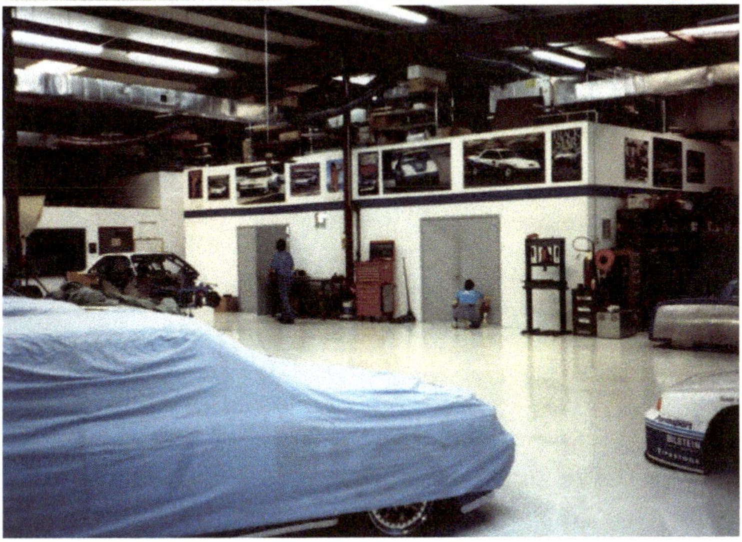

TEAM HIGHBALL
71
mazda
UNOCAL
YOKOHAMA
BILSTEIN

YOKOHAMA AND JOHNSON MAKE HISTORY
The only man to take the 24 Hours of Daytona 4 years in a row
And making YOKOHAMA part of history as the flag comes down.
TEAM HIGHBALL
71
mazda
union
YOKOHAMA
BILSTEIN

© Hayashibara Motorsports Archive

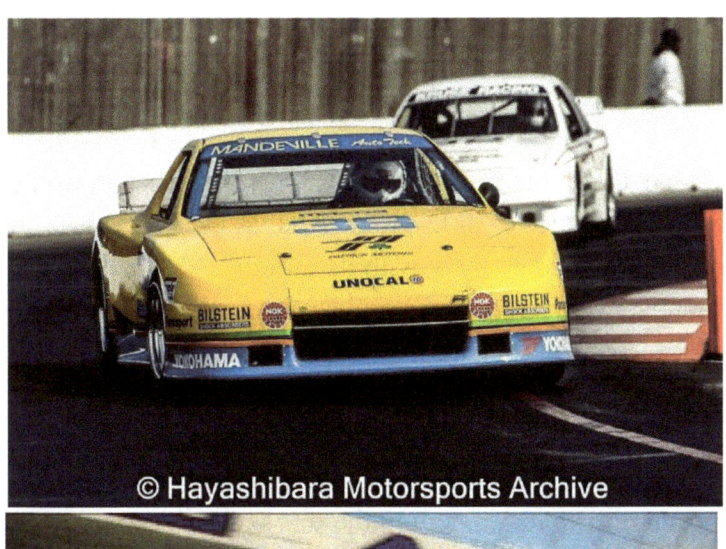

# 11
# Mazda MX6

As usual, the first race of IMSA's 1989 season would be the 24-hour race at Daytona. And, as usual, Team Highball would be there with its faithful old Mazda RX7 number 71. That car had won its class in the past four 24-hour races, and we certainly were going to give it a chance for five. The new MX6 was well underway but would not make it to the track until later. Bob, Dennis and I were executing our endurance racing strategy, running our own race, until Dennis came into the pits saying he could hear a noise coming from the transmission. The best plan was not waiting for it to break but to go ahead and replace it with our spare. That put us behind quite a few cars and meant we would need to drive a bit harder to make up as many laps as possible. At the end of the race, we had finished ten laps behind Dr. Al Bacon's winning RX7, and with the same number of laps as the second place Leitzinger Nissan, that broke down in the last hour. But we were still on the podium. That was not too bad; however, it stopped my string of victories at four, and we would miss out on the big prize money that we were use to having at the first of the year.

The second race of the season was a 45-minute sprint on the streets of Miami and the first race for my new MX6, where I had the fastest qualifying time but some new-car blues and failed to finish. The new car would carry on with my number 71. The old RX7 would race for Team Highball as number 77, with driver Paul Lewis and his sponsor Paul Stanley, bathing suit manufacturer. At the

Sebring 12-hour race, Dennis and I would join Paul Lewis back in my old RX7 for a third-place finish. The balance of the 15-race season, I would be racing the MX6, picking up two victories, Mid-Ohio and Elkhart Lake, for a season-end second place behind Bob Leitzinger's Nissan. Qualifying for Elkhart Lake was interesting; several sets of Yokohama Tires had been flown from Japan for me as a test. I would try each of them and choose one for the race, but for qualifying, there was one special set. Cheech, my engineer, told me I would probably get only one lap with those tires and to be easy with them on a warm-up lap. He was right. I could tell how good they were on the last turn before the timing line; so I really drove hard that one lap and set the pole with a time that would last several years. At Watkins Glen I had a problem with the MX6 and wound up co-driving with Peter Uria in our number 77, yes, our old RX7. We got 2nd place there behind Al Bacon's new Cuneo-built MX6. By the end of the season, Roger Mandeville would also have an MX6 on the track. 1989 would be the end of the contract I had with Mazda to maintain and race cars for them. Dick St. Ives had pulled in all the small support Damon Barnett had set up over the years. There would be only two Mazda factory teams the next year, Roger Mandeville and Jim Downing, whose team would get the most support to race the two new factory-built four-rotor powered RX7s.

 My 1990 racing would begin with a test day at Daytona Speedway. I had been asked by Jim, with St Ives approval, to be one of his co-drivers in the Daytona and Sebring endurance races alongside John Osteen, a good driver from Ohio. The second team car would be driven by

Pete Halsmer, John Morton and Elliot Forbes-Robinson, all top IMSA drivers. Mazda had rented the racetrack in mid-January to "shake down" the new cars and give us drivers a chance to get used to them. They were GTO cars with over 600 horsepower and an expected top speed of about 200 MPH with design work by Lee Dykstra, more car than I had ever driven. After discovering that the clutch wouldn't work in our number 63 car, they sent Morton, a more experienced driver, out for a few laps by pushing the car in gear to get it going. After three laps, he came in, pulled off his right-hand glove and showed us his bloody hand, lacerated from shifting without using a clutch. They looked at me, and I was ready to give it a try. They said I should drive a few easy laps to get used to the car and then read some of the gauges and radio to them the information. When I got to the track, with Bunny and Norm Sanderson, my crew chief, I had a new driving suit but my old helmet and gloves. From the time at Del Mar when I did so much shifting, I had always worn weight-lifters fingerless, padded gloves under the regular fireproof gloves. I was ready to go. They pushed me off, and I found the car quite easy to drive; I had been able, for years, to drive without using the clutch. It's a matter of throttle control that allows the gear change without extra force, and it is easier on the transmission. Drive the car, braking and shifting, reading the gauges by using a toggle switch to move through the gauge readings on the steering wheel, and reporting on the radio. I got it. The car was incredible. When I coasted to a stop, John Morton wanted to check my hand. That was when I became the experienced driver instructing the others. During the 24-hour race, our number 63 car ran a steady pace and was in second place near the end when they put Halsmer, their designated number one, into our car to see if he could catch the leading Mercury Cougar. His car had had a problem and dropped out. We wound up Seventh overall and second in GTO. During the race, while back at the motel for a shower and a nap, I had picked up Lotto tickets to give to each of Downing's crewmen. They were pretty happy with me as their driver.

Back in December I had a call from Peter Uria. If I was driving the Mazda GTO RX7, what about the 71 RX7. Would I consider renting it to him for Daytona and Sebring? I made a deal: he got the car with spares and Evan Whittles, as a crew chief, for a fee. He then found a sponsor and three paying co-drivers, Jim Pace, Rusty Scott and Bob Dotson, and they finished 12$^{th}$ overall and first in GTU for the 24-hour race, adding an incredible fifth win to that car's history. From the winners podium Peter shouted to me: "It's the car!"

There were no GT cars in the Miami race that year; so, for me, it was on to Sebring with the Downing GTO RX7. I was the one to start in the number 63 RX7, and Pete Halsmer would start the other team car from the class number one position. There were three Jack Roush, Whistler Radar sponsored Mercury Cougars, and two Nissan factory assisted 300zx cars along with our two Mazda 4 rotor RX7s that roared off together at the start of the race. Halsmer led from the pole position, and I was there in the mix. It had to be exciting for the thousands of spectators, but soon, my car began to overheat. It was a very hot day, and inside the car, it was very hot. Too soon, I had to pit, and at about the halfway point, our race was over. Halsmer's car didn't make the finish either; he got third place, and we wound up seventh. I was not to be a part of that program that finished the next year with a championship.

At Miami, there had been a GT race in which I failed to finish with my rotary powered MX6; J.C. Negron came up from Puerto Rico to fail to finish in my old RX7. I no longer had a contract to race them but liked coming to Miami for family in the area, However, I did have some more work for Mazda. Dick St. Ives had come up with something for Team Highball. Mazda wanted to know what their 3 liter, three valve V-6 from the 929 cars might be capable of in racing tune. That was a good job for Dennis, our piston engine specialist. I had been doing the rotaries, but he was the one for piston engines. When finished testing, it produced a respectable 360 hp, and we replaced the rotary in the MX6 with it, having to add ballast to meet the regulation weight. That combination would run three races, finishing fourth each time. Then, the 13B rotary engine would go back into the car for sale to someone in California. I would finish my driving for the year with one race in Al Bacon's second MX6 at San Antonio, where I also was "color commentator" for TV coverage of the Pro-Formance sedan race. My last two races would be in a Mandeville MX6 at Lime Rock and a winning co-drive with John Finger at Watkins Glen in another of Roger's MX6s. For the last year with Mazda, I would finish in seventh place, while Roger's two cars finished first and second.

mazda
mazda
IMSA
Cyclo
Firestone
TEAM HIGHBALL INC.
Amos Johnson
O+
TEAM HIGHBALL
71
mazda
BOSCH
UNOCAL
Firestone
TEAM HIGHBALL

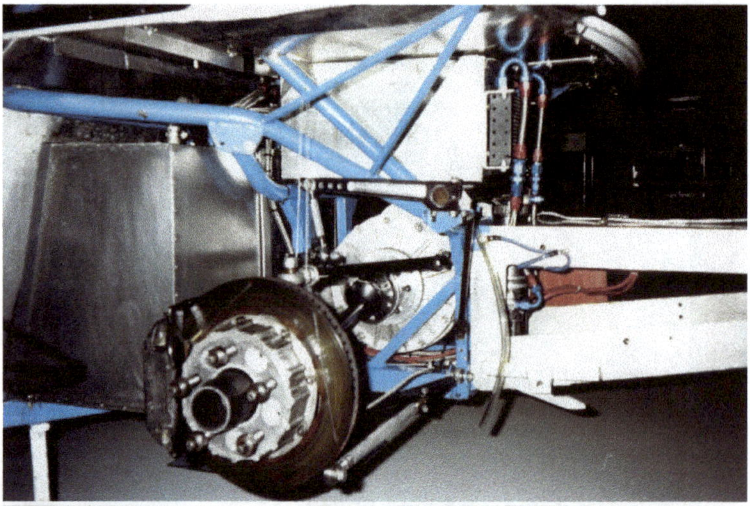

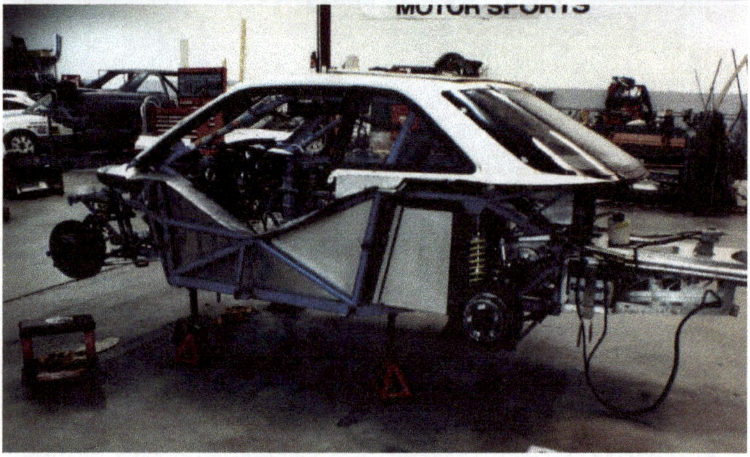
MOTOR SPORTS

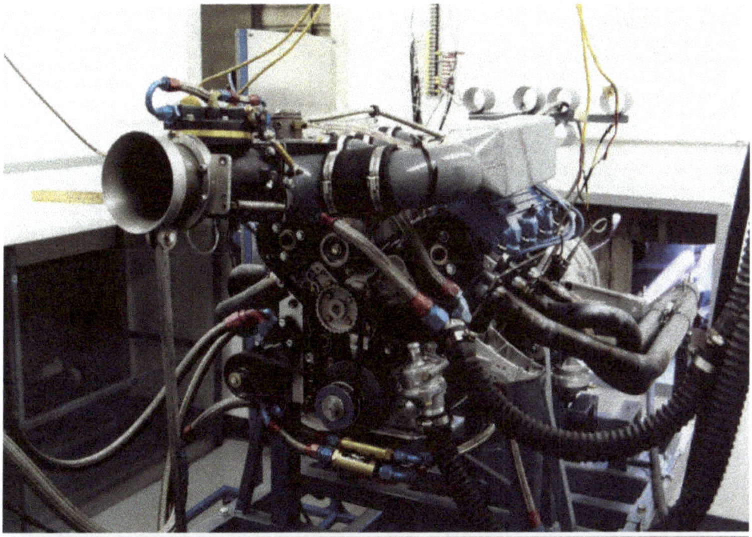

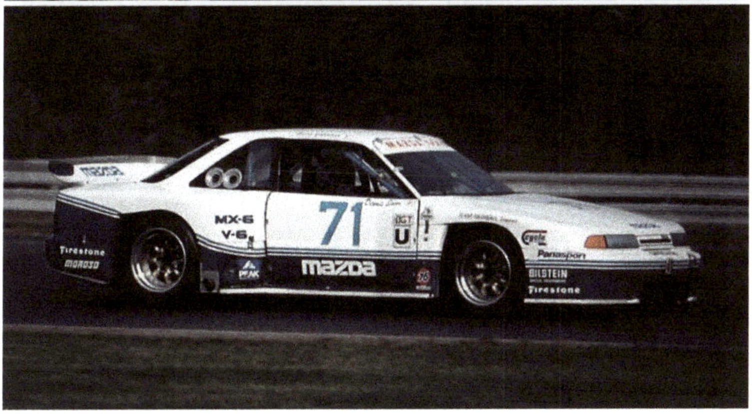
MX-6
V-6
71
mazda
Firestone
BILSTEIN
Firestone

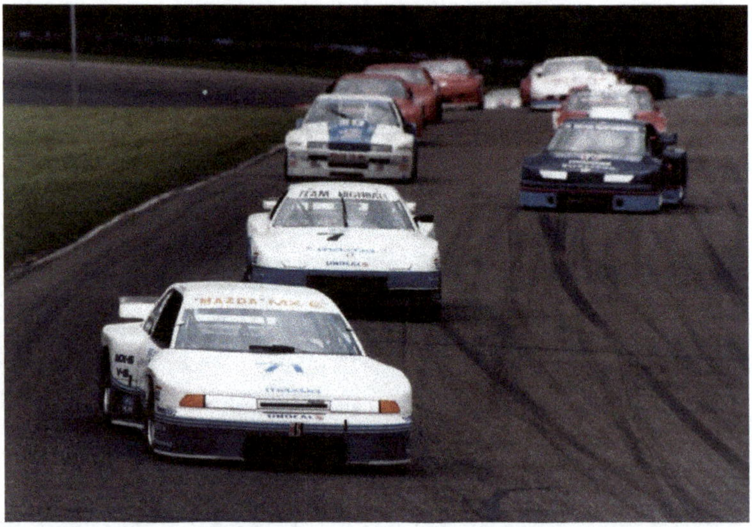
MAZDA

# 12
# Oldsmobile

The Mazdas were gone. I still had my original RX7, but without sponsorship, I couldn't afford to take it to Daytona. Later in the year we would rent the car out for a few races with my Team Highball crew maintaining it. Roger's championship MX6s were also gone, as was his Mazda sponsorship; however, he was still in the rotary engine business and still had a lot of car parts left over. He said we could build a new RX7 and race the Daytona 24-hour one more time. Downing was the only one with full Mazda support for the '91 season with his two 4-rotor RX7s, but he would not be driving one.

I was looking for something to continue my racing and my business and had paid someone to find me sponsorship, and he called to say he had found me a good one, ironically, Johnson and Johnson. They had a new product and would come up with a million to sponsor a top car in IMSA racing; that would mean I needed a front-running Prototype class racer. So, I went shopping and found at Huffaker Engineering in California a Spice GTP with a 650hp Pontiac engine. Spice racecars were very successful, made in England. Let's go racing! I had to get a loan to buy the car, a quarter of the sponsorship, and send our truck for the car. Supposedly it was ready to race, but when we got the car, we had to do quite a bit of work bringing it up to our standards. There was a test day at Daytona in December for cars that would race in the next 24-hour race, and we could make it. My crew was beyond excited, and I was, too. They once had the chance to crew for a Nissan GTP when that team had raced an extra car; so they knew what it meant. I knew well the last driver of the Spice, an old adversary of mine, Parker Johnstone, and he was happy to tell me what he could about driving it. My friend Dr. Al Bacon would be interested in co-driving with me. The test at Daytona was a two-day affair, the first would be for the car, the second would be for me. What a ride; by the end of that second day, I turned a lap only two seconds off the lap record. We could do this.

Back at home, we began disassembling the car to prepare for a 24-hour race when I got the sad news: because of the start of the Desert Storm war, Johnson and Johnson would not go through with the sponsorship. So sorry, team; put the car back together, it's for sale. What a great experience, and what a huge let down. I lucked out and found a buyer in Miami who had a choice of my car or a similar one in England, and I got my money out of it. The car would get a Ferrari engine and go to LeMans in France, where it would have the fastest speed on the Mulsanne straight with Justin Bell driving.

I would visit Roger's shop several times over the winter to see his new car and offer my "two cents" in support and what a car it was going to be. I would drive with him and our third driver would be Kelly Marsh, an accomplished driver from Ohio, past customer and close friend of Roger's. Once at the speedway, our practice times were all within seconds and very close to the class record. Roger qualified in the rain second in class and set the fastest time in the race shortly after the start. The car was running great, leading our class until, during the night, with me at the wheel, a rear brake rotor shattered, stopping that wheel at about 170mph on the back straight. I managed to get back to the pits on three wheels, where the crew had to rebuild the left rear suspension completely. Back on the track, Roger said we had nothing to lose; so drive every lap as if qualifying. We would make up time or break and go home. We didn't have any more problems and finished in third place. The winning RX7 was driven by friends Al Bacon and Peter Uria. In '92 and '93 they would win GTU again, giving Peter his fourth consecutive victory, but not in the same car.

For the first time in many years, I did not even go to Sebring for its 12-hour race, and there was no GT race at Miami. I stayed home and worked on a project car. An old friend and Asheville School classmate from Ohio, E. B. (Ebby) Lunken, had an Argo, Camel Light class, prototype car without an engine. It was a car that had been driven before by Lyn St. James. Our 3-liter Mazda engine from the last MX6 would be perfect for it, and my Team Highball crew would be happy to take on the project to have it ready for the race at Road Atlanta. I enjoyed my first chance to drive a prototype, but in the race, it had ignition problems that stopped the fun. In the Supercar class support race, someone gave me the chance to drive their Consulier GTP, but that only lasted a few laps before it died on track. This Atlanta trip was less than memorable.

Back home in Raleigh, things were heating up. Somewhere along the line I had impressed someone at Oldsmobile with the things I had done building that lightweight RX7, and they wanted to talk to me about a project. The Oldsmobile Achieva was a car that would fall into the GTU category, but it had to use their 4-cylinder, "iron duke" engine. I was interested. They wanted two cars. Scott Hoerr, a driver for them for the past few years, would drive the second car, and I would have a $600,000 budget to build the cars and race in 1992. The engines would be supplied by Marvin Palmer's Bilmar Engineering. OK, let's do it; my shop is raring to go. First, I needed to study the current rule book to see what I can get away with on this car. The Achieva is front-wheel drive with a transverse 4-cylinder engine coupled to a transaxle. Number one: regulations say I can turn the engine lengthwise, any engine from that manufacturer. Number two: the transaxle can be at the rear of the car. With that permissibility, I can design a really interesting racecar. The tube-framed chassis that is required is straight forward, and the rules say it must have a flat steel underpan between the front and rear axles but no other restrictions. My friend Jim Downing has a business in Atlanta fabricating prototype racecars with a monocoque chassis made from one-inch-thick honeycomb aluminum. He would make for me the floorboard, driveshaft tunnel and fuel container as one piece with a flat bottom glued to a sheet of stainless steel. An engineering student at N.C. State College in Raleigh approached me with an offer to do a computer aided design (CAD) program to measure the flexibility, or lack thereof, of the chassis. During the process, he had a few suggestions for locating the roll cage bars and gave me a twist number of 1,200 ft. lbs. per degree, which sounded good. One Sunday morning, he called to apologize; he had put a decimal point in the wrong place for the thickness of the tubing. The twist number was now over 2,000. Thank you. To me, that was enough that if we were able to align the engine's crank up front with the input shaft of the transaxle, there would be no need for "U" joints in the driveshaft. I would mount the clutch, flywheel and starter in the rear connected only by a one-inch tube with splines at each end. All body panels, except the roof, would be made of carbon fiber with Kevlar support bonded to it. The roof and windshield would have to be original. Basically, Team Highball was going to build a whole racecar from scratch.

 I would find that working with Oldsmobile was not as easy as it had been with American Motors and Mazda. I was expected to buy what was needed and then send invoices for payment, and at times, that could take over a month. Also, if I was to receive any outside sponsorship, it would have to be approved by my project manager, and its value would be deducted from my budget. However, any components that Oldsmobile could make for me were free. If I could draw it up, they could make it, and my engineering school classes at Duke University had included draft drawing. Once their shop had made one item, it could be duplicated by their computer aided machine shop for the second car and spares.

 I wanted Hewland transaxles for gearing, and I knew that Dan Gurney had had a problem with the ones that his GTO Toyotas had been using; too much horsepower was breaking them, and he was changing to a different model. I managed to talk with them, making a sweet deal for all their model "F" Hewlands, with complete spares and alternate gears included, for $5,000 plus shipping. My Dan Robson would have to learn everything about them, but I knew my "iron duke" GM engines would not have the power to break them. We would be getting our engines in crates from Bilmar and would never even have one for Dennis to run on the dyno. They were computer controlled, and Marvin Palmer would not give us computer access. We had a "dummy" engine to mount in the car.

Foe suspension, this car was going to have one set-up for endurance races and a very different second for sprint racing. I had been studying the suspensions on formula cars and prototype cars: roll centers, roll couples, instant centers, bump steering in addition to caster and camber, and I was free to take full advantage with this car. I even made some quarter scale models so I could see what was going on. In the rear, I would have inboard mounted disc brakes, and rocker mounted coil-over springs and shock absorbers, all mounted on the transaxle, a huge saving of un-sprung weight. My sprint set-up was with "wide-five" hubs and wheels, saving rotating weight. Everywhere else on the car we would be saving weight and mounting things as low as possible in the car. We were making the braking system so that we could try anti-lock brakes in testing. The things I was working on were being checked by an engineer from GM, Terry Hatchel, who also did work for Roget Penske's Indianapolis cars and the NASCAR Oldsmobile of Harry Gant which was at a shop near us in North Carolina. Terry could fly in, check on us and then visit Gant's shop on the same trip. He was an intelligent, pleasant person who stayed in our home when he visited, and he approved of the things I was doing on our cars.

Since I was now a part of the Oldsmobile racing family, I was invited to co-drive in the Firestone Firehawk series with the Hacker Express team of Paul and Karl Hacker. They successfully raced a pair of cars in the Sport category of that IMSA series. I had known them for years in racing, and at one point, they had sent me a young man to work on my team. John Baines was a student at a special high school in Ohio that would allow him to work for a semester at a job of his choice. Karl Hacker had called to set this up. I would be considered John's instructor and give him a grade at the semester's end. He was a plus for the team and received an "A+" from me. My first chance to drive came in a six-hour race at Mid-Ohio in the touring class Olds Calais, finishing seventh. A week later, I would be in one of their Oldsmobile Quad 442s for the 24-hour Firehawk race at Watkins Glen, NY. I had explained my usual plan for endurance racing and their plan was to have the two of them stay out of cars until they, by rules, had to start driving to get points. That way, they could choose the car in the higher position; the two of them were running for a championship. I would be the first driver and would only drive in the number "0" car. David Lapham would only drive in the "00" car. Buddy Norton, Frank Del Vecchio and Chuck Hemmingson would swap cars where needed until turning a car over to Paul and Karl for the finish. That was a smart way to help the brothers. Fairly early in the race, my car developed a misfire that brought me to the pits for an ignition system change, putting me down a couple of laps to the class. Many hours later, Paul and Karl made their decision and would drive in the "00" car. Sadly, for them, the "00" would have a problem late in the race that would cost them about twenty laps, and my "0" car would make up its lost laps and win the class. It was another victory for my endurance racing record.

We finally finished the first GTU Achieva and took it to the 1992 Daytona 24-hour. It was not tested, and we had problems to work on, but Co-drivers Scott Hoerr, Paul Hacker, and I all got the chance to practice in the car that qualified 6th in class. In the race, Scott and I only completed 89 laps before the engine failed. Back home we continued to work on the second car, and with the Miami street race coming up, it was decided to concentrate on the first car for it. We were able to rent a track in Savannah, GA, for some valuable testing before Miami. Our project manager made the decision to have Scott Hoerr drive Miami, even though he had never raced there, and I had four Miami races under my belt with three second place finishes. That was when we found out that Oldsmobile, as also Dick St. Ives, did not want their drivers to be team owners. Scott would qualify sixth and finish seventh after getting tangled up with another car.

At some point, we were able to take our car to GM's wind tunnel in Michigan for an 8-hour session, and Scott was able to meet us there to help. That was quite an experience, and while we were there, we were able to get the car on a rig that could measure the chassis torsional resistance. The GM operator told us he had never had a car that stiff on the machine. The next step for us was to take the two cars for a test at Mid-Ohio the day before a race weekend would start, where anti-lock brake engineers were anxious to see what we could do. The Hacker brothers had already found a problem with the system on their production street cars. The idea was to allow us to get the cars set for the track, in particular, to choose the gears for those Hewland transaxle for the best performance on straights and turns. Once that was done without anti-lock, we could activate it and see the way it affected our driving and lap times. The difference was amazing. Scott and I both struggled with adapting our driving. Both with and without, our lap times would be within seconds of each other, and we talked about what we were doing. With anti-lock, we would go into turns and stomp the brake pedal, discovering that we would have to then drive on deeper before turning beyond what your mind wanted to allow you do. It was going to take a lot of practice to get the full advantage from the braking. The next day, before practice, the Oldsmobile engineers gave us the bad news. Because they would have to be at each track where we raced, and they had no budget for that, they had to ask us to deactivate the anti-lock system, leaving our advantage in the truck. I was fifth on the grid, and Scott was sixth the next day, but we knew we could have been first and second with our new brakes. No amount of begging would get our project manager to go to bat for us; he was Oldsmobile. Scott wound up seventh, and I didn't finish the race. Our next race, at Laguna Seca, CA, Scott and I qualified seventh and eighth; I finished fifth, and Scott had mechanical problems. We could not run with the Dodges and Nissans. Before the next race, Oldsmobile would cancel our program. There had been a parallel program with a GTO Cutlass team, and they were having more success. Ironically, Scott Hoerr's brother Irv was driving for them. Since we were already on the West Coast, I decided to go ahead and race my car in Portland. Scott, unfortunately, was gone. For qualifying, Marvin Palmer told me that during my time driving a car with his engines, I had never over-revved at any time; so he would use the computer to give me all the power that was possible. I would only get max power for about two laps, but I qualified fifth, ahead of a couple of the Nissans. In the race, I was running a comfortable fourth for a while, staying just ahead of Bob Leitzinger's son Butch in his Nissan. He finally got brave and tried to drive under me in a turn and hit me, knocking me off the track, where I sat without being able to restart my hot engine for the end of my IMSA racing career.

Before that last race, I had been able to race the 24-hour race at Watkins Glen again with the Hacker brothers, where I drove with Chuck Hemmingson, Dave Jolly and Scott Hoerr to a third place. The Hacker brothers won that time in the other car.

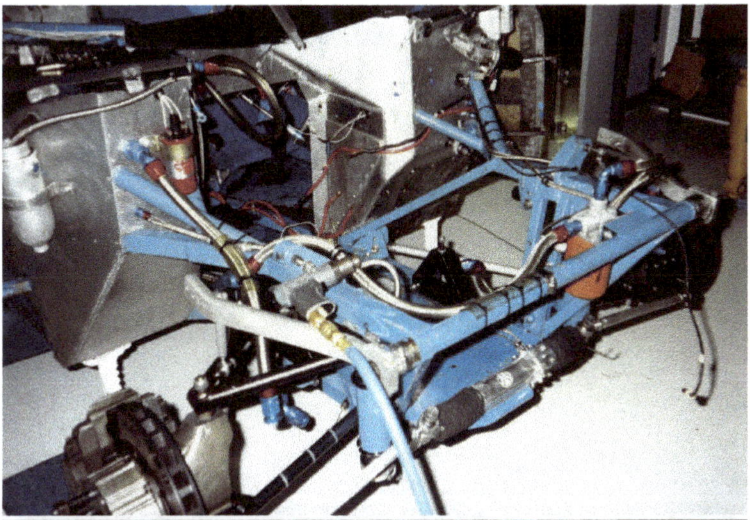

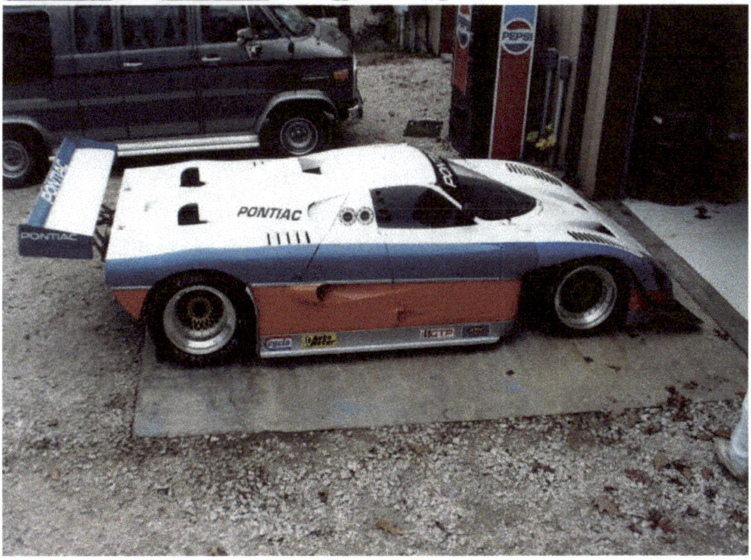
PEPSI
PONTIAC
PONTIAC

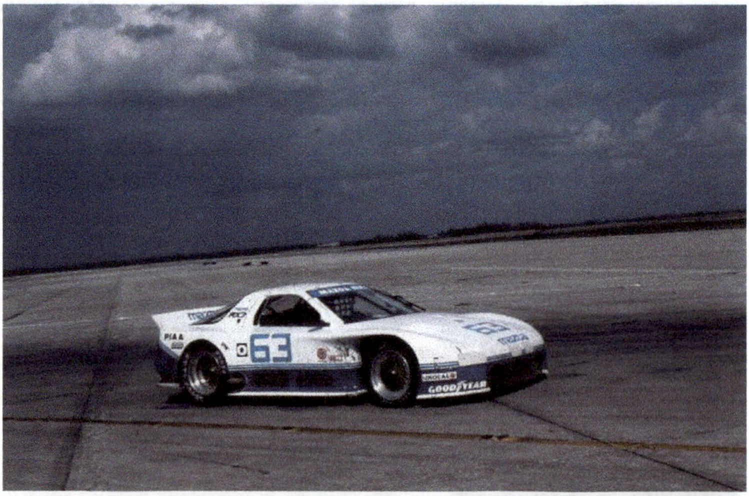
63
GOODYEAR

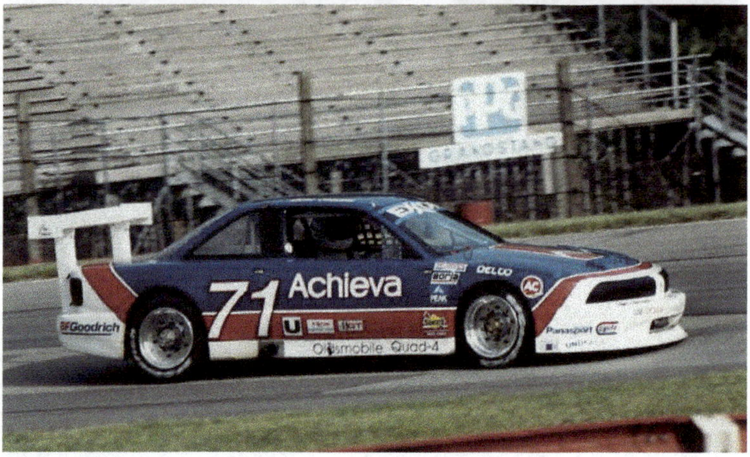
71
Achieva
DELCO
BFGoodrich
Oldsmobile Quad-4

# 13
# IMSA: Technical Director

The 1992 season was not ending well at all. It had been necessary to lay off a few people and cut back our racing to just supporting rental rides, sponsorship had fallen through, and I knew I could not race on my own money. Richard Petty had once said that the way to make a million in racing was to start with three. I just was not ready to give up. I had done some NASCAR races, running well after a learning period, almost winning a race for Bill Ellis up in North Wilksboro, NC. Maybe I could give that another try. Bunny's dad, Jim Dixon, and I drove up to Charlotte to look at a stock car that was for sale, and I found out that I could rent a car and test at Hickory Speedway for $500. I had heard that if you were fast there, you would be good anywhere. Back in Raleigh, I was about to try that when I got a phone call from George Silbermann at IMSA. He had heard that we were closing our shop. What was I going to do? Would I be interested in coming to IMSA headquarters in Tampa for an interview for the position of Technical Director? So, after a talk with Bunny, we were on our way to Florida. It didn't take long to get things in order so we could make a move. Bunny's dad would continue to live at our home, D and J farm, outside Raleigh. The shop, near the RDU airport, would easily sell after it was cleared, and our "get-a-way" place at the coast on the Albemarle Sound we would keep for the time being. It was a double-wide mobile home we had bought after a particularly good racing season back in the '80s. The family enjoyed using it.

We, Bunny and I with our Poodles, arrived in Tampa in our loaded motorhome, towing a car, and found a nice campground. My new job included a company car a nice turbo powered SAAB for me to be mobile while she searched for a home and a place to kennel the pups when we were at the races. We would be at the Daytona 24-hour race right away; it would be my first one as the new Technical Director. It had been a very long time since I worked for someone else, but at Daytona, I found that, without question, I was in charge. I was replacing Jim Woodward, my old crew chief, who had retired back to Missouri. I think that IMSA based their decision to hire me on the fact that I had been running a successful racing team and, seeing that last car my team built, I knew racecars.

Back in Tampa after the race, I would be getting used to the office and personnel that ran IMSA, most of whom I already knew. Mark Raffauf, VP Competition, George Silbermann, VP Administration and John Bishop, CEO and Founder, were all very familiar to me. Mike Cone, Chairman of the board, I had never met and would seldom see. My office was on a second-floor corner where I shared a secretary, Sally Burnett, with Bob Manry, Production Car Competition Director. I would meet with John Bishop right away and find out that my primary task would be putting together regulations for a new category of IMSA racecars to be called World Sports Cars (WSC). I would also be updating their rule book. John said the WSCs should be open-topped, flat-bottomed and cheaper to build. Write the rules! I had just the year before, designed and built a similar car, my GTU Oldsmobile Achieva. Coincidence, maybe not. The open top was to allow spectators to see the driver at work; the flat bottom was to eliminate the molded down-force tunnels and cheaper meant allowing American car builders to compete with expensive foreign, factory-built cars. I was given a year to work it out.

Meanwhile, Bunny had been searching for a home for us to lease in the Tampa area and had found something in the Northern part of the city, a two-bedroom townhome with a fenced backyard bordering a preserve. It was ideal, and we could buy it cheaper than a rental. We backed the motorhome up to its garage and unloaded everything so we could get rid of the coach. We wouldn't be needing it because we would be flying to races, staying in hotels and using rental cars. Once IMSA realized what was available to them, Bunny would have a desk at IMSA and be working with registration and, timing and scoring for the races. We found a nice place out in the country where our dogs could be kenneled while we were gone. Bunny had for years volunteered with registration at the races with Peg Bishop and the IMSA registrar, Peg Gilman, who later would be dating IMSA's Chief Steward, Marty Kaufman. I would work closely with him at the race tracks.

For the 1993 season, I would put out a quick set of rules and begin the WSC class by allowing some existing cars to be modified to race for class bonus money. As my old friend, Charlie Rainville, had done, I would be available to help competitors modify their GTP cars. All of this would be done while attending to technical aspects of the other IMSA cars. For help at the races, I hired my old partner, Dennis Shaw; we worked well together. Dennis had been my first hire and my last employee; for his retirement, he would get to keep all of the shop machines and equipment, including the dynamometer. He still has a racing engine building business. Some of the European car builders would be contacting me as they began work on their WSC racecars, wanting to know what my rules meant pertaining to different areas. Ferrari would telex their questions to me, and I would answer, sometimes giving them advice. When their first car arrived in New Jersey they flew me up to see the car so they would know it to be acceptable at its first race. Spice Engineering in England was constructing cars for WSC also. For engines in these cars, I had set rules to equalize the power output using displacement and car weight to balance performance.

Part way through the season, John and Peg Bishop would take their leave from IMSA; it had been their life, and they would be missed. They had grown it from a 12-car race in Alabama to a worldwide organization. Bunny and I had been witnesses to the whole development. Maybe it was appropriate that we were here for their departure. IMSA was getting a new CEO, Dan Greenwood, who came to us from the Riverside Raceway in California, and he knew racing. He and I got along well; Bunny and I would take him fishing in Tampa Bay on our 23- foot Sea Ray boat. I had traded that Firehawk Mazda RX7 racecar to a friend from Chicago, Ron Tambourine, for the boat. I sent the car North on the Mandeville truck, and Ron sent the boat South with his brother when he was coming to St. Petersburg on business. If you were going to be boating on the Bay, you needed to take a class with the U. S. Coast Guard Auxiliary. Bunny and I did and found that they were such a good group that we joined; before long, we were helping teach those classes.

One morning, Sally told me Dan and Mark wanted to see me; so I go over to Dan's office, and they had come up with an idea for me to go to Daytona before NASCAR's next race and work with their tech crew as a chance for me to see how they did their car inspections. I liked that, and Dan would call and arrange it. I went over, got credentials and worked with their tech crew checking the cars. It was a good experience, I was received very well and drove back to Tampa that evening. Monday morning when I got to work, I was met by Dan: "What the hell did you do over there?" I was at a loss for words. Apparently, NASCAR had disqualified several top cars, including the pole sitter, after their qualifying session. I explained that they had a piece of equipment that could "sniff" for an air leak and had never yet used it. I had explained to them how I would use the "sniffer" to search for ways that a team might try to get extra air around the restrictor plate, which they used to manage horsepower. It turned out that was exactly what the teams were doing, and NASCAR caught them. A bit of respect was gained all around.

At the racetracks, Dennis and I gained the respect of not only the rest of our IMSA workers but the racing teams as well. We were knowledgeable and helpful. I remember seeing something on a car that was illegal. I could have simply held the team accountable, but instead, I showed them how they could accomplish the same in a legal way. Things like that would help our credibility. We were all connected by our radios, Marty Kaufman in the tower and the pit marshals, Dick Martin, Sue DeWeaver, Bob

Raymond, Barry Fletcher and Sam Holland, to name a few of the regulars. We had code names or numbers, and there was continuous chatter so that we all knew what was going on. Marty and I connected very well; for example, he would ask me to talk with the drivers on the first row of the start, explaining how we wanted to see the start done. As an Official I was accepted well because I had been both a driver and a team owner.

Dan had another project for me. One of the auto manufacturers wanted to build and race a car using liquid hydrogen as a fuel and needed to know if we would accept it to race at the 24-hour race at Daytona. With safety being the main concern for the car, I would be sent to England, to the Spice car builder, and make that decision. The Chrysler Corporation would pick up all expenses and make reservations. For me, it was just a few days' work in England, and I was comfortable with that, I could drive on the wrong side of the road quite well; I had raced on all the road and even shifted gears with the wrong hand before. I had reservations at "The Bear", a well-documented, historical lodging, and I had been there before when Bunny and I had been on a tour a few years earlier. A Chrysler representative would meet me there to make sure I was properly cared for. At Spice, I met with the engineers who were responsible for this new car and also with a technical director from the FIA who was representing the LeMans 24-hour race. The car was interesting; it would have two 500hp electric motors hooked to a generator that would be powered by a small helicopter engine modified to run on liquid hydrogen. I was assured it was not a bomb. Now, many years later, we have cars driving on our streets with similar set-ups. The FIA representative and I agreed to accept that car to run our races in a "demonstration" category. So, now I need to get home. I was running as fast as I could to the airport in my three-cylinder Peugeot, windshield wiper flopping in the breeze as I drafted other cars in the London mist. At Heathrow, I stepped up to a security checkpoint guard, presented my papers and answered his questions. Afterwards, he said: "Mr. Johnson, I also do some writing for a sports magazine, and I know who you are. I would love to know what you are doing in England". I told him I was very sorry; he would have to find out later. As it happened, the project never came to fruition.

However, the WSC project did come along well, and the next year, 1994, those new open topped, flat bottomed and less expensive cars would race for the IMSA Exxon Championship. FIA and Europe would soon accept them, and they would truly become World Sports Cars. Before the start of the season, I would go to Detroit to hold a meeting with representatives of the manufacturers that would compete in the new Exxon Supreme GT series. They would gather for a meeting at the GM offices of Herb Fishel. As we started, Herb greeted all and then stopped. Looking at me, he said: "I'm sorry, Amos, when I look at you, all I see is MAZDA". I assured him that I was now IMSA and promised I would treat all fairly. It was a good meeting, and we were ready for the season's racing.

It was a new year, new sponsor, new cars and a new Chairman of the Board (CEO) and President (COO). Charles Slater had bought IMSA after racing for a few years with us. He and a friend had developed and patented a disposable medical syringe and sold it for millions and he used some of his money to buy the racing organization from Mike Cone. A businessman and friend, Hal Kelley, would be named President; gone was my friend Dan Greenwood. We had a couple of new marketing VPs in the offices, but all operations would continue as before. Charles Slater would continue to drive in our races, promising that his being the owner would not have any effect. However, early in the season, at a pre-race drivers meeting, where he was introduced as the new owner, he told everyone that if they ever had any problems, they should come to him, and he could take care of them. That statement got to me. Mike Cone had been a great owner. If the business was good, he stayed out of it. Not only was Charles the owner, but he was also racing in it and now offering to control things there. In retrospect, I may have been rash, but I told him that he had just taken my job away and I would resign. He came to my office, closed the door and asked what he could do to change my mind. I told him that if he got a racing person for president, like George Silbermann, I would stay. And when he said he couldn't do that, I told him I would continue until they found someone to replace me. It was a good part of the year before Bunny and I headed back to North Carolina. Oh Yes, George would wind up working for NASCAR and then even for the FIA.

# STAFF

**IMSA STAFF:**

|  |  |
|---|---|
| Chairman of the Board | Mike Cone |
| President & CEO | Dan Greenwood |
| Executive Vice President, Competition | Mark Raffauf |
| Executive Vice President, Administration | George Silbermann |
| Vice President, Television | Joe Weidensall |
| Director of Operations | Tom Seabolt |
| Technical Director | Amos Johnson |
| Production Car Competition Director | Bob Manry |
| Race Director* | Marty Kaufman |
| Communications Director | Lynn Myfelt |
| Director of Special Projects/ Testing & Certification | Bruce Clarke |
| Assistant to the President/ Office Manager | Christine DeRobertis |
| Comptroller | Wayne Coffield |
| Director of Scoring | Ron Smith |
| Operations Manager | Chip Couzens |
| Marketing Accounts Supervisor | Tracy Serdynski |
| Administrative Assistant | Pam Fitzgerald |
| Licensing/Membership | Sally Burnett |
| Entries | Becky Swilley |
| Secretary, Marketing | Francine Schoel |
| Communications Assistant | Christine Baldwin |
| Reception/Secretarial | Maria Trippe |
| Production | Wayne Coffield, Jr. |
| IMSA Truck | Henry Copeland |
| Chief Timer & Scorer* | Barbara Smith |
| Registrar* | Marolyn Rogers |
| Official Starter* | Jim Sidley |
| Pit Steward* | Bob Raymond |
| Assisting Race Officials* | T.J. Bishop, Sue DeWeaver, Barry Fletcher, Sam Holland, Norman King, Dick Martin, Gina Pattison, Butch Peloquin, Bob Rogers |
| IMSA Announcer* | Bill Bowser |
| Assistant Announcer* | Greg Creamer |
| ARROW/Yearbook Editor | Ken Breslauer |

*Race Staff Only

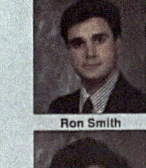

Mark Raffauf  George Silbermann  Joe Weidensall
Tom Seabolt  Amos Johnson  Bob Manry
Marty Kaufman  Lynn Myfelt  Bruce Clarke
Christine DeRobertis  Wayne Coffield  Ron Smith
Chip Couzens  Tracy Serdynski  Pam Fitzgerald
Sally Burnett  Becky Swilley  Francine Schoel
Christine Baldwin  Maria Trippe  Wayne Coffield, Jr.

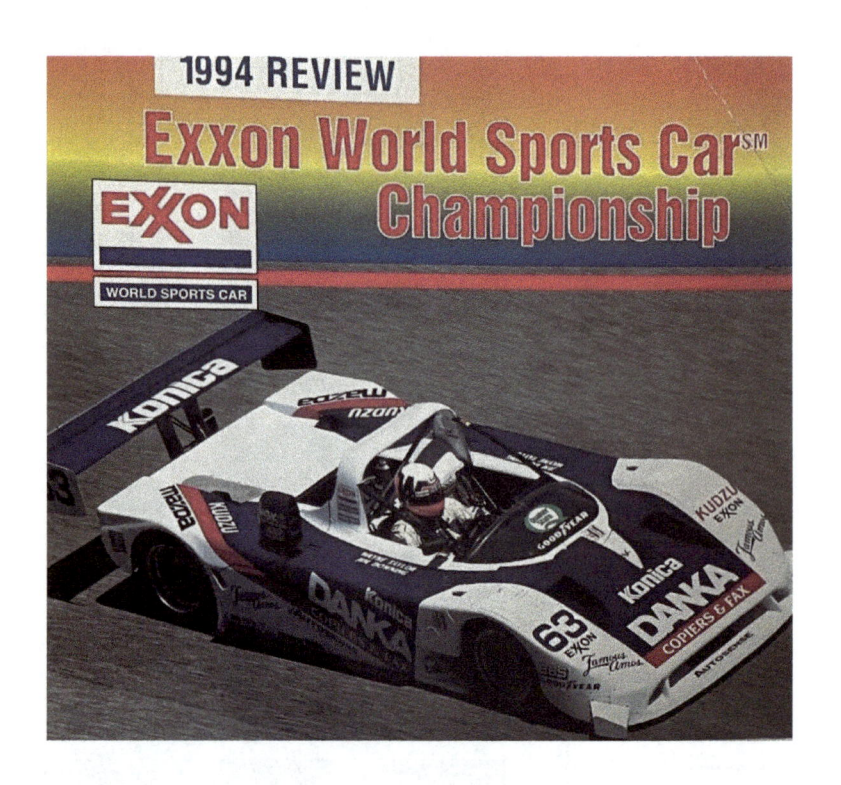

# 1994 REVIEW
## Exxon World Sports Car Championship

# 14
# NATCC

It turned out to be easy to sell our townhome in Tampa; a young doctor coming from Duke to intern in Tampa loved the place. She had a dog and liked the fact that when she came home late at night, she could just drive into the garage and close the door behind her. We packed up and headed to Soundside, the name we had given to our get-a-way place in Columbia, NC. We built a dock there with the help of Bunny's whole family and always invited them to come when they could to enjoy the peaceful place. It was just a few miles from the little town of Columbia and not far from the historic town of Manteo, site of the Lost Colony. I always thought it funny to see the highway sign "Lost Colony one mile". Our place was right on the water of the Albemarle Sound, with a few houses and a lot of wildlife. There was one place with a bit of a tower within a cluster of cypress trees that belonged to the government. At times, the Navy's F-14 and A6 jets from Norfolk, VA used our area's waters as a bombing range, dropping flower filled bombs on radio-controlled boats that were speeding in an oval pattern offshore. They were controlled from the neighboring tower, and we were always warned if the range was active. I was fishing just offshore in the fog one morning and got the warning, a screaming F-14 at an altitude of maybe a hundred feet right over my head. When finished, the plane would fly along the shore, low and slow, wagging its wings. I had seen the pilot wave to me at times. We had a boat ramp built into our seawall for launching our small sailboat and our 23-foot Sea Ray speedboat. One time, some of the Navy personnel walked over to ask if they could use my boat ramp to retrieve a boat with a bent propeller. It had hit an underwater stump, bending the prop shaft. It was a beautiful craft made of dark wood with hard wooden covers for the open cockpit. They were usually launched from the ramp in town, but this one would have taken hours to get back to that ramp. I asked if the powder bombs had ever hit a boat and was told "close enough" was a good hit. Since we didn't have yet a screen porch, Bunny and I would build a big one ourselves. We were happy and comfortable there and much closer to family in the Raleigh area.

I did get one more chance to race in IMSA. A North Carolina team with an RX7 asked if I would co-drive with them at Daytona and Sebring in 1995. Ralph Thomas and Doug Campbell had a car built by Joe Carr and wanted help for the endurance races. I had a few things left over from Team Highball that I could contribute to the effort, a racing speed jack and a radio system for pit to car communications. I remember the Sebring trip well. Bunny and I drove down in our Chevy Suburban to Tampa before the race to visit friends and had our car stolen there with my helmet and driver's suit in it. By the time we worked things out in Tampa, we were a bit late getting to Sebring. Ralph and Doug had already been practicing and I was told their lap times were about eleven seconds behind the GTU leader. Ralph told me to take the car out in the last practice before qualifying and see what I thought. I drove two laps and came in, telling their young crew chief to swap the rear tires, side for side, and I went back out for about three more laps. When I came back in, Ralph said we were now only one second behind and I should drive in qualifying. It bothered him that I went that much faster than him in his car, but I tried explaining that when I first accelerated, the car pulled to the left, and when I let off the gas, it pulled to the right, telling me that the right rear tire was taller than the left. That is called "stagger", and for that track, the opposite would be better on the fast righthand turns out on the airport runways. It helps you to understand more about what is going on with your tires. You have four patches of tire tread that the car sits on, and they have three things to do, accelerate, brake and corner. Those tires can only give you 100 percent of their traction; therefore, if you ask a tire to do two of the three at the same time, you are splitting the traction. If turning while braking or accelerating, the tire cannot give you the best of either one. Also, if one tire loses traction, you no longer have the maximum that your car is capable of. For the best braking traction, the car must be well balanced side to side, and the brake pressure adjusted for front to rear stopping without lock-up. Then you cannot have maximum stopping if you are turning or shifting gears or have a wheel off the track or on oil or sand. When you downshift while braking for a corner, you must ease off the brakes when you let the clutch out, or the rear tires will lock up. The result there is that you just gave up some of your front braking. Don't let the clutch out until you are ready to get back on power. You can even downshift multiple gears before getting back on power. Anti-lock brakes are the best answer. That Joe Carr Mazda was plenty fast, and I was very familiar with the Sebring track, having raced there 27 times before with 4 wins. We had some engine problems in the race and did not finish. Ralph wanted to know if He rented a track somewhere, could I teach him to go faster. And the answer was yes. Bunny reminded him that he was a building contractor for a living, and I was a racecar driver. Actually, I did a lot of driving instruction; several organizations had driving schools, and I helped them when I could. I had been invited into the Road Racing Driving Club (RRDC) back in the '80s and instructed in their school at Daytona. There was a school group, Track Time, that rented tracks in the South, where you brought your own car and received instruction. At one of those schools at Rockingham Raceway in NC. I took the chief instructor, Dr. Bill Gurley, for a ride in his Saleen Mustang; on the first day of classes, only instructors were on track. He was so impressed that he suggested all instructors should have me take them out in their own car. I had a great time and drove about a dozen different cars. During that school, my stepson, Tad, drove a MX6 Turbo that Mazda had given me, but he was not my student. However, the morning of the second day, his instructor came to me and said I should take him because he was already faster than him. At another one of those Track Time weekends, at Charlotte Motor Speedway, my stepson, Corky, was a student. He drove in that red RX7 that Damon had sold me and would go on to get a racing license from SCCA, but he never aspired to a career in racing. On another trip to a school in Charlotte, I had been requested as his instructor by an NC Ferrari dealer in his twin turbo V-8 GTO on racing tires. He asked that I drive him around the track for a few laps because his hands were going to sleep after a couple of laps; I showed him he could be driving with just his fingertips on the wheel instead of a death-grip. When he asked me how I was so much faster between the infield turns, I asked him if he had the accelerator to the floor. Someone asked how I could drive that million-dollar car laps on a racetrack. My answer was as if it were mine.

One morning, after about a year at Soundside, the phone rang. Roger Elliot, someone from Tampa that I had met through racing, asked me to meet him as he passed through RDU airport, which I was able to do. He had an offer for me. He needed a Technical Director and Competition Director for a new racing series that he was starting in the U. S. that would be based on Europe's successful Touring Car Championship. He had a money man, Gerald Forsythe, to back him. They wanted to get American manufacturers involved, and I would be the perfect person for the tasks. Name recognition was one thing Roger had to be aware of; there are not many "Amos Johnsons" out there attached to automobile racing. My dad was one if you were involved with medicine. There was always the Famous Amos chocolate chip cookie man, but my name could open doors now or get someone to answer the phone. When racing at Lime Rock one time, we had a new "want-to-be" racer show up for our race, Walter Peyton, of football fame. Just before the morning drivers meeting, I thought it would be good to meet him; so I stuck my hand out and said: "Hello, I'm Amos Johnson", and his response was: "Yes, I know who you are". That was the first time I understood how far I had come from the small town of Garland, NC. Before I could respond to Roger, I had to talk to Bunny; I could only consider it with her blessing. After explaining what I had been told, her question was where we would be going, because she was not interested in moving to Detroit or California. Their office would be in Tampa, I told her, and she was ready to start packing. We really liked the Tampa Bay area, and this time, it would be a permanent move. If we sold Soundside and the D and J Farm, we would be free to go anywhere. D and J farm didn't grow anything but poodles, but it had been part of a large farm at one time. The manor was built in about 1914, and we had bought it along with 23 acres of land, three other homes and various out-buildings that had been a part of the farm. One old house came with an occupant, the daughter of a slave that had been granted life-long privilege to live there; when she died, we tore that one down. Another house with no running water or wooden floors, we donated to the local fire station for training, and after they burned it, they cleared the land where it had been. The third home was good enough to keep as a carriage house, and our son, Whit, lived there for a while. The old Manor was special. We found an architect who would rebuild and modernize it, and we hated to leave it, but we found a local realtor to work with. He wound up buying the place for himself.

Down in Florida we wanted to live not too far from Roger Elliot and his wife Kathy, and hopefully closer to work than when we were there before. So, a realtor showed us several places, and we chose a gated community just off Tampa Bay that had a fresh water lake connected to the bay. There was a dam separating the waters and a boat lift to get out to the salty water, and that meant we could keep the Sea Ray in the water at our dock. It was a very nice set-up and not far from a Catholic Church that we would join.

Bunny was a "cradle" Catholic and had gone to grade school at a Catholic school in Raleigh. We had been married in my ancestor's protestant chapel in Ingold, NC. Back in the 1700s Thomas Johnston, Jr. had left Ireland for religious freedom. In Raleigh, we had found a small Catholic Church to join, and after fifteen years, we had our marriage blessed there. So, we found a church near our new home and would be very happy to be a part of it. I would go there for the program to become Catholic. Ironically, on a trip through my old home area in Eastern NC, we visited Ingold and found that the Johnson Chapel had become El Iglesia Catholica de San Juan, How appropriate!

    The North American Touring Car Championship (NATCC) office was only ten minutes away. Roger and Kathy were from Canada and had brought with them a delightful writer and PR person, Tom Hnatiw. Roger would hire a local, race-oriented operation officer, Jon Lewis. That was it to start. We had connections in Europe, and Our financial support, Gerry Forsythe, had connections to CART, the Indy Car organization. The master plan was to be a support race at Indy Car races with cars that could be bought from Europe and cars that would be built here in the United States. That was where I came in.

    First order of business, Jon and I would go to England for a couple of races, on consecutive weekends, Silverstone and Thruxton, to see how they conducted the races. On the week in between we would visit a shop to see how the cars were built and cared for. The officials there were very accommodating, allowing us to go where we wanted and meet their teams. We expressed interest in helping our teams purchase year-old European cars.

Between races, we visited the Renault Formula One shops, where one of the touring car teams resided; their cars were very much like IMSA's International Sedans, just a bit larger and more powerful. I drove over there, and upon returning home, Bunny and I took a vacation to the Cayman Islands for some SCUBA diving. So, for 19 days, I drove on the right side of the road, quite well, I might add. Back home I was having to carefully adapt to the other side.

  My rule book was coming along, the problem being equalizing competition between the year-old European cars and our freshly built American cars, notably those from the Dodge factory team, who would have Mark Donohue's son, David, as a lead driver. I had several meetings with teams and sponsors before we had the first race. About twenty cars made it to the race. Dodge Stratus, Honda Accord, Toyota Carina, Ford, Mercedes and BMW were some of what showed up to race in 1996 at tracks like Lime Rock, Detroit, Portland, Toronto, Mid-Ohio, Vancouver and Quebec. We used a standing start, as the Formula One cars did, instead of a rolling start, and I had to build and control the starting lights. Bunny was involved as our registrar and in timing and scoring at the track. We had for our Chief Steward a very experienced Canadian, Terry Dale. We were a small group, but we got the job done. Racing alongside the Indy cars of CART, we had a good season with David Donohue as our year-end Champion.

  The second season started well, but there was not much of an increase in the number of participants, and the fans didn't seem to be as enthusiastic in America as they were in England, where Touring cars were the main show.

Here we were in support of the Indy Car series, and Gerry Forsythe warned us that '97 might be our last season. And it was.

Bunny and I had made the move to Florida as a permanent change, and, as a 57-year-old, I felt it was for our retirement to Florida. Bunny's sister Kitty and her family lived in the Ft. Lauderdale area, which was not that far away, and over the years, we had made friends outside the racing community. We had become involved with the Coast Guard Auxiliary for Tampa Bay through their Boating Safety classes. That would become, for us, a new adventure.

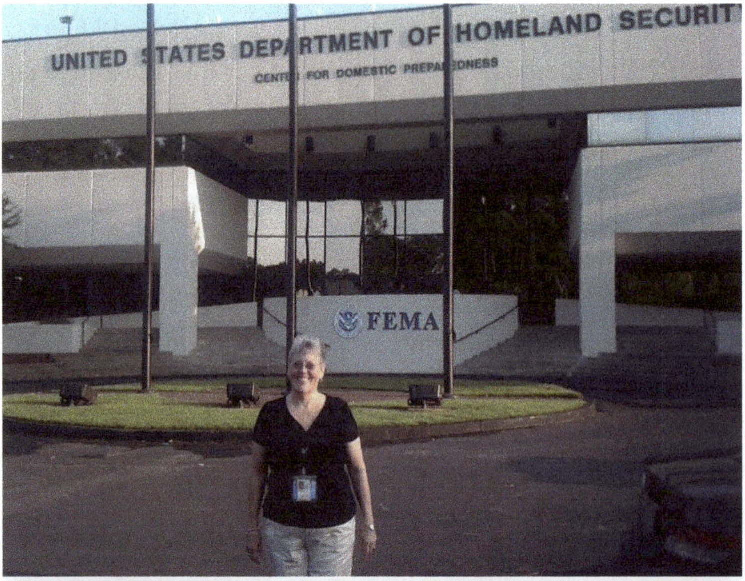
UNITED STATES DEPARTMENT OF HOMELAND SECURITY
FEMA

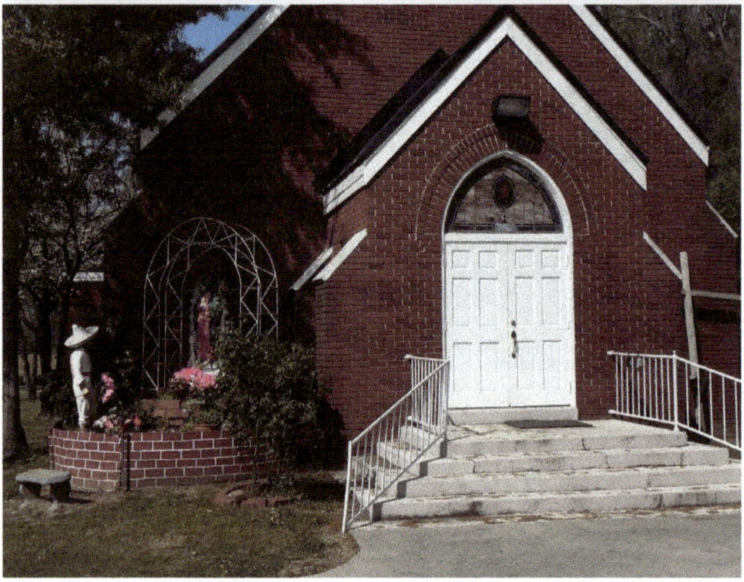

# 15
# Rest of Story

The U.S. Coast Guard had roughly 40,000 members; The Coast Guard Auxiliary had about 30,000 volunteer members to help the Guard. Across the country, there are Auxiliarists in Areas, Divisions, Districts and Flotillas everywhere, there is water, offering boating safety classes for the public and assistance to the Coast Guard. Tampa Bay is a very busy boating destination, and Division Seven, with as many as nine Flotillas, is extremely active. Bunny and I joined Flotilla 79 back when we first came to the Bay area and took the classes they offered. In a short time, we found ourselves instructing the classes, going on missions and taking positions within the organization. Bunny was Information Systems officer and the first in our area to enter mission information by computer, for which she got an Auxiliary Commendation ribbon and certificate. I would be able to teach all chapters of the boating course and even go to San Diago to learn a special class for the Auxiliary and the Coast Guard members. If a Cutter was coming into port, they could arrange with me a time for the class. I also specialized in charting and navigation. Over the years, we both had to learn to operate in the Coast Guard computer system. We both also became operational as Coxswain and Crew so that we could do boating missions in our boat as a facility for the Coast Guard.

A younger neighbor of ours, Robin Bonanno, who happened to race cars in the SCCA, came to us saying that her mother wanted to move from New Jersey and liked our home; she would buy if we would sell. Years later, I would go with Robin to test tracks to help her drive faster, and she would win multiple SCCA Championships. We were not in love with the home there, and it would not be an immediate transaction. A few weeks later, while Bunny was visiting her family in NC, I stumbled on a place that was an interesting possibility, about five miles away, in a suburb of Tampa, Oldsmar. The home was on a bulbous part of the Bay to the North called Safety Harbor. It was an older place with two additions over the years, and it had an oversized garage with a workshop and a second garage door on the water side. I liked that. It also had a swimming pool and pier out back. With Bunny's approval, the deal was done, and we would live there for the next thirteen years.

Ransom E. Olds, on a winter trip to Florida from Detroit, had found this area at the top of Tampa Bay and bought 5,000 acres for a winter home. Back then there were no bridges across the water between Tampa and St. Petersburg, and the people would have to drive up through his new town of Oldsmar and then down to St. Pete, an all-day trip at the time. He built a service station and rest area, eventually a country club. That was where we would be, just walking distance from R. E. Olds Park. Bunny and I would add lifts on our pier for our new 31-foot Trawler and 19-foot run-a-bout boats. Our lives were very much involved with the Auxiliary. Ultimately, I would be Division Seven's Commander and Bunny, Flotilla 79's Vice Commander.

But, during that time, in the year 2000, the phone would ring again. Bill Boye, Asheville School classmate and longtime friend had found someone near his home in Vero Beach, FL, who had bought a new Corvette to race in the SCCA's Motorola Cup series. The man, Reed Knight, didn't want to drive; he was wealthy and just wanted his business to sponsor a car. His business was Knight Armament Corporation, making guns for war. Would I be willing to help them get the car up and running? My help would be my connections and test driving. Now, it is amazing how many old Asheville School students from my time there have wound up in racing. Bill Boye and Ebby Lunken had parents that raced. Russel Norburn and I raced together in early IMSA, and the Fountain Brothers, Bubba and Reggie, raced boats. There were two earlier students that had raced in SCCA. Grover MacNair, who was our partner in the street shop, would also be a racer and had gone to The Asheville School.

 I connected the team with Marvin Palmer at Bilmar for the Chevy V8 engine, ADDCO for sway bars, and Koni for Shock absorbers. They would handle all the work, and I would not see the car until we tested it at Daytona. I did need an SCCA racing license, which would come after a phone call to the SCCA president, Nick Craw, an old IMSA adversary. Of the 30+ cars at the test on the first day, I was first on the timing sheet. Bunny asked if there was anything else I had to prove. They wanted me to drive the race with Randy Pobst, a Florida native who I knew as an excellent driver. Randy said for me to do all the testing; if I liked it, he was sure he would too. For that first race, in qualifying, a wire fell off, causing the throttle to disconnect, and I idled around the whole 3.6- mile track for a last place starting position. I would be first to drive in the race and would pick my way through the field to 19th when there was a yellow flag caution. Cars re-grouped for the restart. We had been told in the drivers meeting that they would use the infield flagging stand, just before going back on the oval, for restarts instead of the Start-Finish line on the front straight. The pace cars lights always go out before a restart. When we got to the infield stand, I saw the green flag and I hit the gas and started passing the slow cars, which had not accelerated. I passed all 18 cars, going onto the back straight in the lead and saw the confusion in my rear-view mirror. Those guys must have been asleep in that meeting. My friend Bill Bowser, the track announcer, was going wild: "Amos Johnson just passed all those cars and took the lead, last to first!" Unfortunately, our pitstop was miserable, and we finished eighth.

The Sebring race would be better, but not easy. After qualifying, the officials found that our car was still running on leftover Daytona gas instead of the gas available at the Sebring track. Guess where I had to start? Work would be cut out for me. I can only remember two times in my over 400 races where I crashed on the first lap; so I was trusted to be the first driver. Bill Boye watched the first lap from the top of a truck and was trying to count how many cars I passed; a lot. By the time I turned the car over to Randy, I was in ninth place. He would take it to the lead before being beaten to the finish by an old competitor of mine, "Little" Joe Varde, in his Dodge Viper. Second place was not too bad for my last race ever; Randy and I were on the podium and would go home happy.

We stayed busier in Tampa Bay than most other Auxiliary Divisions. The Coast Guard from there covered the whole Caribbean, on sea and in the air; plus, we had MacDill Air Force Base with U.S. CENTCOM running the wars from there. We were the envy of all other Auxiliary units for the things we did with them. On September 9, 2001, we had planned a simulated disaster involving a small cruise ship, the Coast Guard, the police and a hospital, and the Auxiliary was to help. My trawler would pick up a TV crew for coverage because they could film from the upper deck. They boarded early, and we were having coffee and donuts on the way out to a rendezvous point in the Bay when the TV crew asked if my TV worked out on the water. We had just turned it on, and I heard someone say they thought it was a live picture. There was a skyscraper with a fire near its top. As we watched, an airplane hit the neighboring building. I had one Coast Guardsman aboard, and I told him to get on the radio back to his base. Our simulation exercise was definitely over, and I started dropping people off wherever they wanted to go because our mission was cancelled.

After that, we began taking missions all around MacDill, night and day. The Coast Guard equipped us with special equipment like night vision binoculars. I even set up a special small boat training for the military after their security group came up with some "flats" fishing boats and mounted 50 caliber machine guns on them. Our membership soared, people wanting to do anything to help. That would go on for a long time. When the Republican party had their Presidential Convention in Tampa, our division was tasked with protecting all bridges in the Bay area from possible terrorism. We stationed crewed boats beneath the bridges 24 hours a day for four days with a home base at Flotilla 79; Bunny and I ferried meals out for the crews. A few months later, I was back at MacDill, representing the Auxiliary, when President George Bush paid CENTCOM a visit. I sat in the small bleachers directly behind the Bush brothers; Jeb was Florida's Governor. Air Force One had pulled up in front of our open hangar to unload. It was an impressive sight.

While doing all of this I was becoming more involved with boating. I became a marine surveyor, and, between studying and taking classes, I managed to become a Coast Guard Licensed Master Captain. Three of us Captains started a business, Bay Area Captains, to help the people of Tampa Bay with anything boating. If you were new to the area and bought a boat, you needed our help. Bunny and I had joined a Boat Club earlier, not a fancy one, but just friends and neighbors. One new neighbor bought a nice boat and ran aground his first time out; he hired me to take him out and show him where he could and couldn't go. If you boat in Tampa Bay, you will run aground. If someone says they didn't, they are lying. I did. The same man came back later, saying his brother-in-law was coming to visit and he would need to take him to a restaurant by boat. He had me show him several choices by water, and he paid and fed me that time. I would be the leader of flotillas of boats going to Destin, FL and another time to Key West.

I had heard that the Coast Guard Academy in New England had a three masted sailing ship that they used to train the cadets, the *Eagle*, and during the summer, there were two positions on board that could be filled by Auxiliarists, Navigation Instructor and Captain's Cook. Whereas I am not a good cook, I am a good navigation instructor. I applied, and in 2004, after an extensive interview, I got the job. Bunny said I would never experience anything like that; so I should go for it. It would be a six-week cruise starting from Boston, and we would be in a port each weekend so the public could visit the ship. The *Eagle* had been built by the German Navy as the Horst Kessel in 1938, along with four others, and they were taken by the Allies after the war. She was quite a vessel: a 300-foot long, wooden Barque, square-rigged with three masts and 22 sails, and we did sail with all sails up most of the time. Hauling sails was a training job for the about 200 cadets, but at times, I would go aloft with them. They would like me for that. I was also a quartermaster-of-the-watch, at times responsible for running the ship at night while the Captain slept. Navigating and charting was where I had most often dealt with the cadets. The regular crew numbered 36, including us two Auxiliarists, and a few guests would at times come along. A highlight of the trip was sailing into Halifax, Nova Scotia, with Bunny and our grandson, Dean Diggett, on the dock. They had flown up for the weekend. The two of them left for home and I cruised on for a couple of more weeks. We always were watching the weather and saw that there was Hurricane Charlie, headed toward Florida. As it got close, I worried because it sure looked like our home in Tampa was its target. Our Captain said if I could find a way, I was free to go home, but there was no way to get there in time; so Bunny would face it without me. However, all our Auxiliary friends would step up to help prepare. When the storm turned in early, we all breathed a sigh of relief. My six-week adventure was soon over, and I would be back on the Bay again.

While living in Oldsmar, I came up with another hobby, acting in little theater. There was a group, Oldsmar Players Art League (OPAL), that was putting on plays, and for the play Twelve Angry Men, they needed twelve men, so they recruited me. It was fun, and I was not afraid to get up in front of a crowd because I had done that often as an instructor and when I showed the "plan" for Amway. I once had an Amway business and even helped them set up their business in South Africa. I would wind up doing about six more drama and comedy plays, but Bunny wouldn't let me do a musical. I tried out for a role in a movie that was being filmed in our area, but someone I knew got the part.

Our last big Auxiliary task came along when I got a call from The Coast Guard Master Sergeant in St. Pete. A military group at CENTCOM had approached him to get some boat training, and he had to tell them that they should call the Auxiliary for small boat training. He then gave them my number. I would speak with a Colonel whose team was an army version of a Seal Team. He had bought them blow-up boats and quiet engines so they could be air-dropped anywhere for a mission. They were 19 of the sharpest young men you could imagine. I picked four instructors to work with me to do the custom training; four of us had been in the military. We had to teach navigation and charting for sure. After the first class I told them they would each need a GPS. Next class they all were wearing them on their wrists. The Colonel said they would get anything I thought they might need. As a graduation test, I came up with a mission for them. They couldn't use their boats but could use ours. They would simulate being dropped into the Bay in different locations at night, with a bridge in another part of the Bay being the target. They needed to plot their course and speed to all arrive there at the appointed time. They all passed, and their Colonel was pleased and invited us over to their unit at MacDill for a cook-out. I was unable to go, but my people were happy; they even got to go to a range and shoot some of their weapons. I had been away doing some FEMA training.

After The Hurricane Katrina disaster around New Orleans in 2005, FEMA realized that Coast Guard Auxiliarists had been doing some of the same training courses that they required of their disaster responders, and friends of ours had been involved. They convinced us to join FEMA. We would be paid about $20 per hour even while training. We heard that there would be interviews over in Orlando and called for an appointment. As It turned out, Bunny and I were the first ones interviewed for a new group that would be called their Surge Fource, the first ones into a disaster to set things up for the response. There was a lot of training, even though we had done a lot of the on-line courses through the Auxiliary. Training would be in Alabama, Pennsylvania and West Virginia. Travel plans were handled for us and we each had a government credit card. You never took a personal vehicle because you could be redirected or extended as needed. At home, you kept things planned for 48-hour call out. At one point, we were trained to do the callouts. For example, we were training in Anniston, Alabama, when a tornado came through the area. Since we were already there, they would change our orders to let us handle it, and we would then call up the help that was needed for that disaster. Bunny would be on the government computer system doing it, and I was helping figure out who to activate. When we were training on the government's computer system, we were in the mountains of West Virginia, where we were told that if we heard helicopters, we should stay inside. There was an underground facility for our President there in an emergency. The worst event we ever dealt with was for the storm Sandy that hit New York and New Jersey. They called us and said go to Trenton, NJ. Four hours later, they said stop. We want you in Pasadena, California, the day after tomorrow. They had an unused building with computers and phones, and we would be working there for almost three month with only two days off; however, we would be on the West Coast, working East Coast hours, 200 of us at time, overtime and double time, through Thanksgiving and Christmas! It goes without saying it was interesting and profitable.

We would do 21 years of Auxiliary and five years of FEMA. At one point Bunny had made an investment and had a home built in Lehigh Acres, a community near Ft. Myers, FL. The idea was you start building and then sell it before the home is completed. A friend had done that and put quite a bit of money in the bank, but our home was not complete or sold when the market crashed in 2007. By 2011 we had decided to sell the Oldsmar home on the Bay, finish the one in Lehigh acres and have a paid-for home for final retirement. Since you can't just stop everything, with help from new neighbors Steve and Cathy Lowery, we opened a jewelry shop, Bun's Bling, on-line and in a flea market nearby. I also found a job as a volunteer Deputy with the Lee County Sheriff's Department; for five years, I drove my patrol car virtually any where I wanted to, waiting to be called to a crash scene where we would be directing traffic. There was a computer in the patrol car, and I would learn to use their system and radio for communications. With GPS, they knew where I was, and I knew everything going on in the county, "10-4, good buddy". That was a great way to learn where everything was in the County at their expense. But when my boss found out what I had done for a living, I got one more task, teaching the regular Deputies how to drive fast in their Ford Crown Victoria patrol cars. He had sent me out to a private airport used by the Sheriff's aviation unit to meet the deputies who did the training class. They had five old Crown Vics with steel bumpers that were used for the Pit maneuver training. Three of them asked me to pick one and come out to play with them, and they roared off. What fun! We chased each other and bumped each other for half an hour until the boss said I was hired. I set up a course on the runway using traffic cones, and the Deputies had to chase me through that course. Then, I would let them catch up so they could bump into me, spinning me out. No one ever caught me on their own, and it was fun for all of us. I had developed a spinal problem over the years requiring surgery, and I would be unable to be on my feet, directing traffic, for long periods of time. I had enjoyed being a part of the Sheriff's Department and hated having to give it up, but after five years, it was best for me to stop.

  With time on my hands no job to go to, I would turn to my computer. From a family history booklet compiled back about 1940, I knew that the Johnsons immigrated from Scotland, through Ireland, to Eastern North Carolina. That would be my next task. I joined Ancestry.com, sent off a

DNA sample and was on to my next adventure. It has been several years and quite a trip. But because my sister's kids want to know about the family, and she died of cancer back in 1988, I would write a family book. Finally finished, I have found that writing is a great hobby, and since so many people have asked me to write a book about my racing adventures, here I am doing it now. I hope you enjoyed my book.

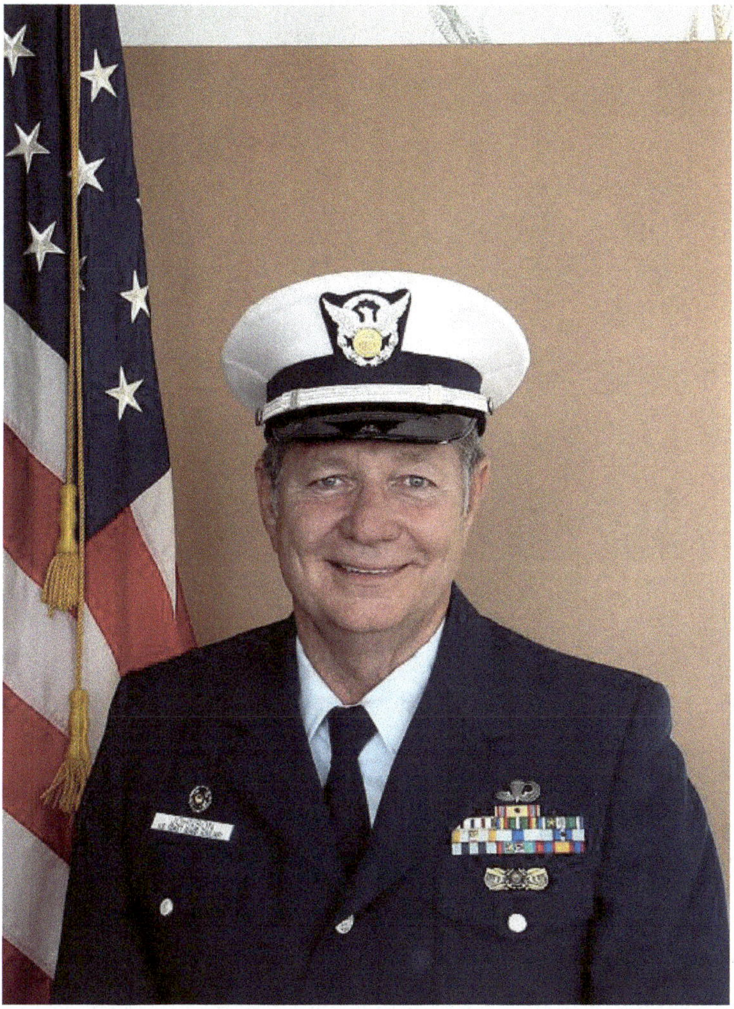

*U.S.C.G. Barque EAGLE, America's Tall Ship*

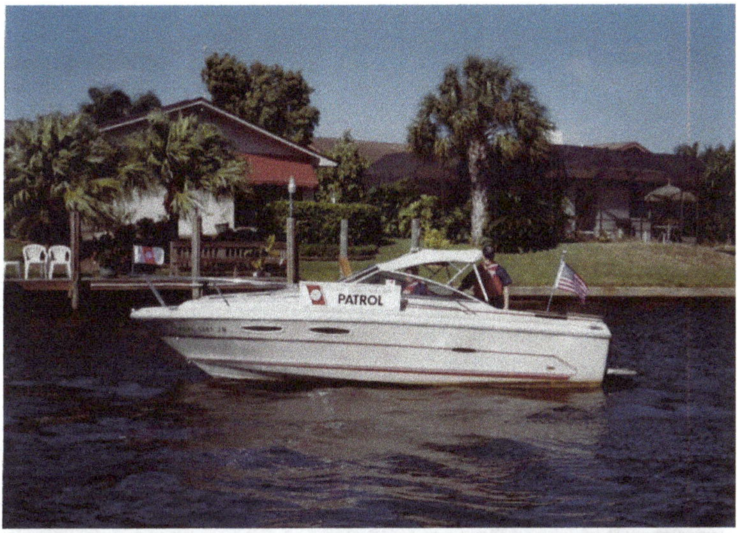
PATROL

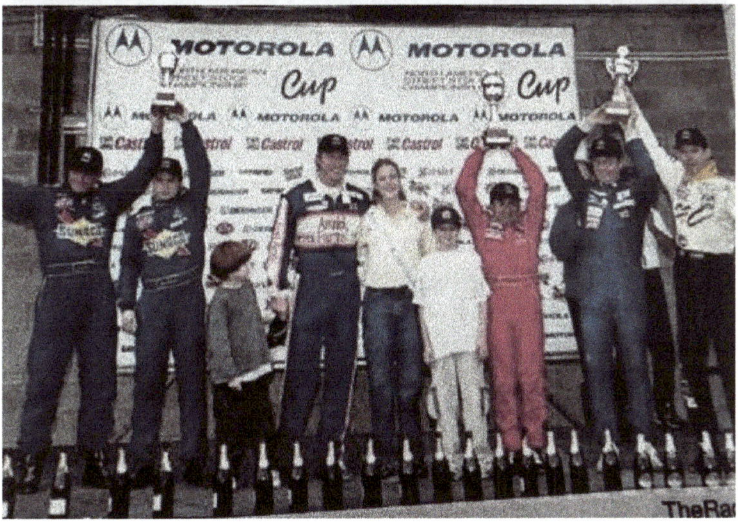
MOTOROLA
Cup
MOTOROLA
Cup
Castrol
TheRa

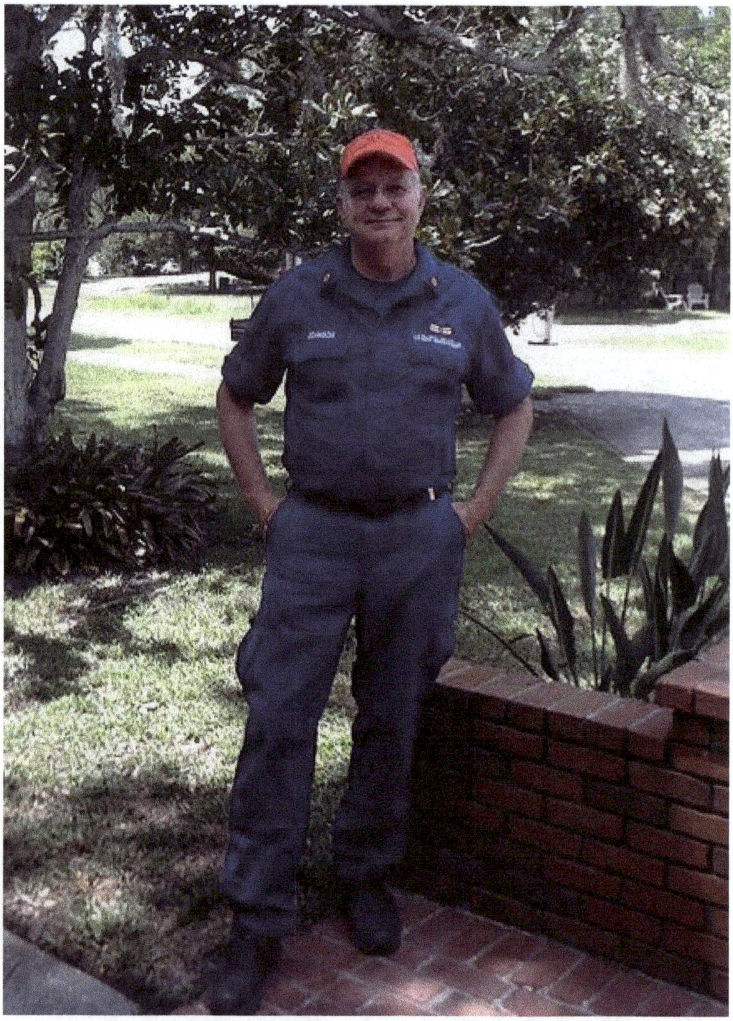

# 16
# My Career

It was time to call it a career. I raced for 38 years and over 400 races with 41 professional wins. IMSA may say only 39, but there were two mistakes in their yearbooks. Six of my victories came in 24-hour endurance races. I raced in 19 of the 24-hour races, and only once did I fail to make it to the finish; that must be a record in itself. I believe Peter Uria and I are the only ones to win the same category four years in a row; my four came in the same car, one that my team had built. No one has accumulated more championship points in IMSA.

Daytona is my favorite racetrack. Over the years, I raced there 73 times with 12 wins and 30 times on the podium. There were 42 top 5s and 63 top 10s with only 9 DNFs. I believe the only drivers with more wins may be Hurly Haywood and Bobby Alison. For many years, we would be having our Thanksgiving dinner in Daytona just before IMSAs finale weekend races.

Sebring is the race I enjoyed the most. I started going there in 1960, and I started working at those 12-hour races in 1961, timing and scoring first and then as a pit and grid marshal. I even took leave from the Army to go to the Sebring races. I started racing there myself in 1970 and ran 29 races, with my last one being second place in year 2000, my last race. That is 40 years of going to Sebring, Florida, for the races. The 12-hour endurance race is harder on car and driver than 24 hours at Daytona. Of my 29 races at Sebring, 16 were the long ones, with 3 victories and 7

DNFs. I won only one of the shorter preliminary races. About 17 of Bunny's birthdays were celebrated at Sebring; the race there is always at the same time in March. One year, for a birthday present, she got a flight in the Good Year blimp.

Through racing, Bunny and I would get two trips to Europe and three to Japan, and I would get an additional one each without her. IMSA and NATCC races took us many times to Canada and gave us many coast to coast runs in the USA. One trip in our motorhome was four races in five weeks around the country, with the middle weekend off in Jackson Hole, Wyoming. The only state we have not visited is Alaska; we don't race dogsleds. An interesting race weekend came in 1987 when I raced in Texas and Connecticut on the same weekend. Half the crew took my Mazda 626 to Texas for a race on Sunday, and my RX7 went to Lime Rock for a Monday, Labor Day, race. Bunny and I flew overnight so I could drive both. Twice, Bunny and I were in the same race. In the first IMSA GT race at VIR, she finished second in class driving with her boss, Paul Fleming, in his Fiat, where Roger Mandeville and I won. She also was in a Team Highball Gremlin at Mid-Ohio at the same time I raced my Gremlin there. I am sure she was IMSA's first female driver.

For about 20 years, I was provided with a car, or sometimes two, by my sponsors, AMC and Mazda. The way Oldsmobile worked, just before my car reached 5,000 miles, no matter where I was, I had to trade it in with a dealer so it could be sold at a discounted price as a "program" car. If it was a car I liked, I could then buy it at that lower price. Yokohama always provided passenger car and truck tires for us, as did B F Goodrich. My Levi Strauss sponsor benefits extended to all my clothes, except underwear, for nine years. My pit crew's uniforms were Levi's, of course.

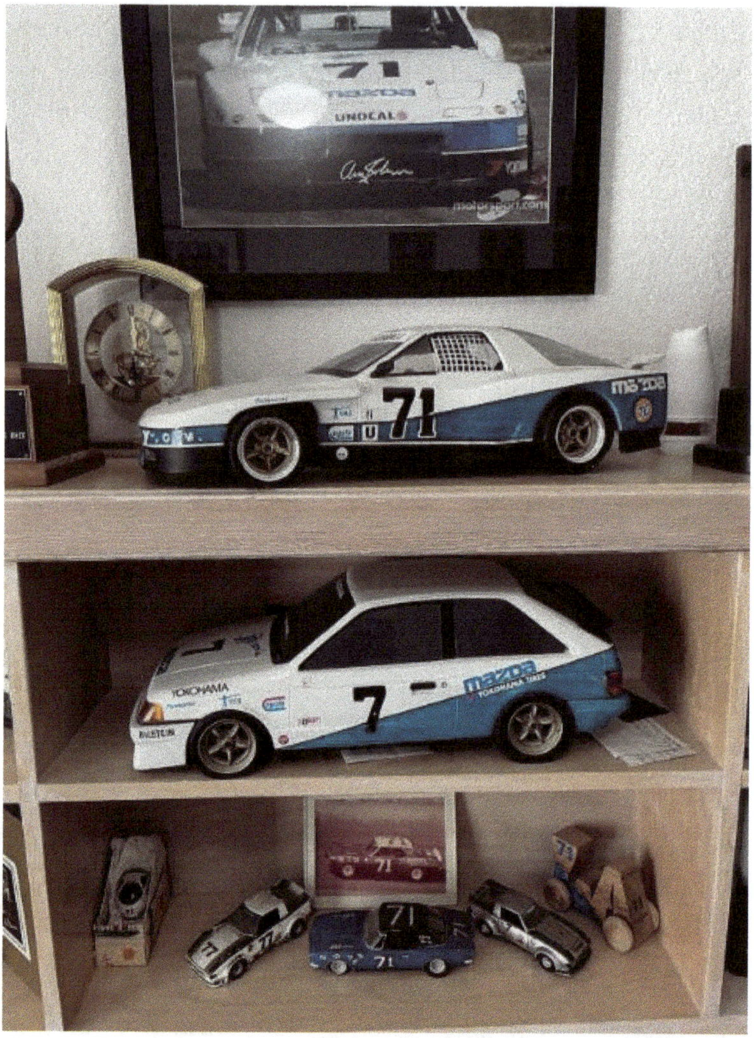
71
UNOCAL
71
7
mazda
YOKOHAMA

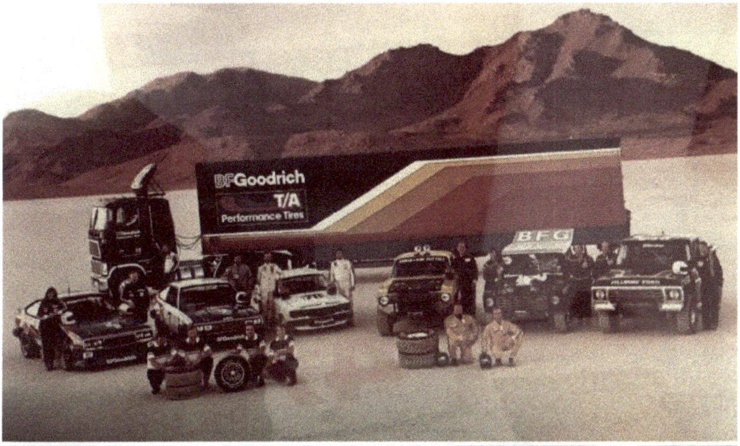
BFGoodrich
T/A
Performance Tires
BFG

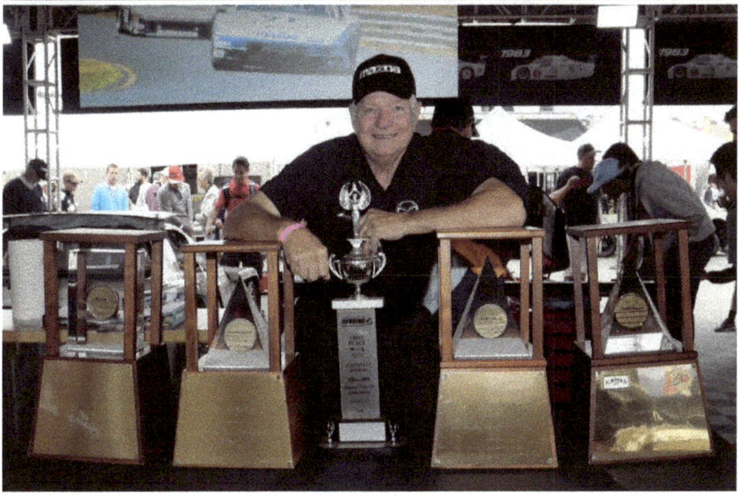

Division 7
Presents To
Amos Johnson
With Appreciation
For Dedicated Service as
Division Commander
2010 - 2011
AMOS AND BUNNY JOHNSON
IN APPRECIATION
FOR YOUR HELP IN CREATING
THE FUTURE OF
PROFESSIONAL SPORTS CAR RACING
FROM YOUR FRIENDS AT IMSA
IMSA
Division 7
Award of Appreciation
Presented To
Amos Johnson
For Expended Effort For The
Benefit Of The Division
Far In Excess Of What
Would Normally Be Expected
2006

# Photography

Photographs from Amos Johnson collection and Dennis Shaw collection. Pictures by Mark Yeager, Hal Crocker, Jerry Howard, Mark Windecker, Joe Hayashibara and Chuck Ritz, courtesy of IMSA, B F Goodrich, American Motors, Mazda Motors and Oldsmobile. Artwork by Roger Blanchard.

Milton Keynes UK
Ingram Content Group UK Ltd.
UKHW020810141124
451205UK00008B/508